BEAUTY FOR ASHES

LaDeema Burns

ISBN 13:978-1514824672

Dedication

First of all, I am dedicating this book to my Lord and Savior Jesus Christ, without whom I would never even dare to dream! To my wonderfully made husband that God tailor-made just for me, I thank you for loving me unconditionally and never finding any fault in me. To my two wonderful children that God blessed me with, you have been my two angels, encouraging and supporting me in everything I do. God has shown me His Great Love in trusting me to be your mother. To my Mom and Dad who I love so much, through you, I have learned a greater love and forgiveness. To all the wonderful people that God has placed in and through my life that are gone home to be with our Lord, my step-dad (his mom and dad), grandma and grandpa, my other grandma, my biological father's mother, I thank God for all that each of you have imparted to me to make me the woman I am today.

I really want to thank God for placing the angels in my life who have been instrumental in helping to fulfill the Word that the Lord gave me concerning writing this book. To my wonderful and priceless sister in Christ Monisa, who God sent into my life that has been such a wonderful gift and token of His Great Love, there are no words that can express my love for her, how she has been there for me every step in this journey.

I pray for every person who reads this book. May the Lord Minister His Love and Healing to you as you read. May you embrace the blessing that no matter where you have been or where you may find yourself right now, God has a Great and Mighty Calling on your life to touch and Change lives around you. This is book is especially dedicated to those of you out there who feel that they are not worthy, feel abandoned, rejected, trapped, sexually and physically abused, are in bondage to drugs and sex, and whatever else that may be holding you down. Some of you feel like there is no hope and I am here to say there is! God has a plan for you or you wouldn't be here right now. As soon as you can fully surrender to Him, He will take the ashes of your life and make His beautiful masterpiece out of you and your life, so you can share how amazing our God is. I pray who ever reads this book God will do his prefect will and plan in your life! God bless you always!

Part I - Ashes

Part II- Beauty

Ashes

A Broken Family Tree

People all over the world are in search of discovering their true identity. "Where did I come from?," or "From where did my family originate?," are common questions that drive us to either live for a purpose or to use our family's woes, vices, and strongholds as an excuse to barely exist. The family tree has been used throughout the ages to help us trace our roots. In fact, its origin is biblical. Someone 'begat' someone else, who 'begat' someone else and the generations continue. The Bible's accounts give us a history of where we all came from, and thus a family tree has been created.

I'm not sure if I'd link my family history to a tree. After all, a tree is constructed of roots and branches that are connected to its trunk. My background would resemble a tree with pieces of broken branches that have been chaotically misplaced and then glued back together. For a long time, I lived under a dark shadow because of the stigma associated with a dysfunctional and broken home. I later learned that God had a Plan all along, but as a child, my world was upside down and inside out. For me, dysfunction and chaos were the everyday norm.

Most little girls have a childhood filled with Barbie dolls and doll houses. Their minds are full of vivid pictures and imaginations of what they want their lives to be in the future. Their 'Knight in Shining Armor' is picture-perfect. He can be characterized as tall, dark, handsome, and filthy rich. He's portrayed as romantic, loving, and very strong. He is there to be your Superman that will destroy the villain and save the day. Living in a world filled with fantasies offers an escape from reality, a safe haven from hurt, and the hope that dreams really *can* come true. My childhood constantly required an escape of the reality called 'my life'.

As a little girl growing up on a farm in Indiana, life was sweet. I especially loved the sense of family and togetherness that farm-life offered. My grandfather owned, maintained, and worked very hard on the farm. Grandpa was my Superman. He was a very strong military man, an outdoorsman, and a man who had a work ethic that was unmatched. Grandpa's everyday job was at an auto factory, where he then returned home to run the farm. He taught us all there was to know about being self-sufficient, such as: gardening, canning those foods, hunting, butchering those animals, and trapping them for fur. I admired grandpa so much and greatly enjoyed helping my grandmother pack his lunch every day. We could never part ways without exchanging a kiss on the cheek, for him to express this token of love, a reminder to me that I mattered. These early-life experiences gave me an appreciation for the simple things in life that I would soon forget.

In spite of the happiness I experienced on the farm, my family was very much broken. My household consisted of me, my mother, her boyfriend Paul, and my baby brother Jimmy. Paul entered our lives when I was just over a year old, and Jimmy was only a few months old. Shortly after, mom's sister came and took Jimmy, in an effort to try and raise him away from our household. Then, just a few months later, Mom and Paul got married. I can still recall the day that I got to visit Jimmy at my aunt's house and told him that we were siblings while outside during playtime. I was actually about nine or ten years old and my aunt sternly warned me that if I ever said anything about it again, I would never see him again. The mere thought of not ever being able to see my younger brother of 11 months again sparked a tremendous amount of emotional turmoil for me.

Now back to my atypical family tree. My *biological* parents were first cousins. Yes they shared blood, as their fathers were brothers. My dad's name was Raymond, and he left my life when I was just a few months old. I did not understand that my dad was my mom's cousin until I was older, but I always knew that Raymond was my father. I would not learn anymore as to what happened to my dad until one day when I was in third grade my mom gave me a letter that he had written to me when I was a baby. In this letter dad poured his heart out to me, explaining why he had to leave when I wasn't even old enough to talk. When I read the letter, my nine year old mind had the enormous task of trying to process so many emotions at once. There I was, forced to process all of these adult matters and emotions while most nine year olds are trying to figure out what children's games they were going to play with their friends after school., Considering that he and my mom were so closely related, it would definitely stand to reason that he was ostracized, criticized, and humiliated by the family and anyone else who knew the truth of them having a child together. Rather than with his voice, from his own hand is how he expressed his love for me. Even though his sentiment was expressed on that paper with pencil, it was indelibly etched in my heart. For years, I held that paper in my hands and cried each and every time I read it until there were no words that I didn't have memorized. I tried to preserve it for as long as I could, but eventually, the letter and its words faded away as I didn't know if I would ever see my father again.

The Art of Self-Preservation

Children have the amazing ability to bounce back. They are resilient, and even with bumps, scrapes, and bruises, children fall down and get right back up again. It's like the saying goes 'fall down seven times, stand up eight'. Somehow, in some way I learned how to keep picking up the fragmented pieces of my life and move on the best way I knew how. Although I was deeply wounded, I managed to function the best I knew how. Life at home with Mom and Paul did not make my absence of my biological father as a child any easier. I witnessed a great deal of physical abuse and drug-induced violence between the two of them. It was quite the norm for them to go out to the neighborhood bar and hang out all night, leaving me now without a caring mother either. Their relationship was so volatile that my wellbeing was often neglected.

In the midst of all that transpired during this time, I can recall that the Hand of God was the only true comfort that I had in my life. God was there from the very beginning, blessing me as a healthy newborn even with so closely blood related parents. Looking back through a family album one day on the farm and seeing a picture of Paul holding me in his arms, showed me again how much God had lent a helping hand in my early life. In the pictures I was wearing a cast on both of my legs. Come to find out later on, I was born with a hip ball socket disorder where one was larger than the other. The cast started right above my knees, had a bar that connected my legs at the knee and then the rest of the cast went all the way down to my ankles. I can remember how difficult it was for me to walk, but I managed to get around and how I would often use the bar as my dinner table. I was followed by a specialist for several years at the Children's Hospital where he told my parents that I would not be able to walk by the time I reached my early twenties. However, a year later, during my check up, the doctor said that I was doing great, and that whatever I was doing to try and become a normal little girl should be continued. God had helped heal me and had shown again that he would have a very large presence in my utterly imperfect life for many occurrences thereafter.

As I think back to the times when I saw that photo of Paul and, I remember seeing a smile on both our faces. Although I had seen that picture numerous times, I never thought to ask Mom where the picture was taken. When I finally broke the question, I wished I hadn't, as she told me that he had been locked up in prison at the time the photo was taken. I could not fathom how or why he was in such a place. This was 'Dad' to me, as he was the only father I knew up to this point in my life. My little heart broke at the thought of someone so hard-working, loving, and caring being locked away. Later on, I found out that he had been in prison because of drugs, but even *that* could not change my mind about how wonderful he was to me. I loved him dearly, and that's all that mattered to me because I simply did not want it to be any other way.

As soon as 'Dad' got out of prison, we left the farm life with my grandparents and moved into an apartment. I thought this was the start of a new life, a happy resurrection to a family I so dearly wanted. Some fond memories were made in this apartment, including a birthday party I had that Jimmy came to, even though I didn't know that he was my brother at this point. There were also some memories that I wish were never made; ultimately terminating my thoughts of a new happy life in a new home. I can still vividly recall one incident where I saw Mom and Dad fighting. When they had this fight, Dad was recovering from back surgery and was wearing a brace. I remember seeing him in such pain lying on the floor, begging Mom for help, but she refused to help him get up. I wanted to help him, but I was too little. I felt helpless and I yelled at Mom, "What are you doing? Why won't you help him? He's hurt!" I'm not sure what the fight was about, but this was the norm and only one of the many times that I had witnessed the violence between them.

Growing up in this type of environment was like a breeding ground for the enemies to plant seeds in my mind that would later be used to try to destroy me. It was only by the grace of God that I did not end living in foster care, prostituting in the streets, or dying way too young. My parents leaving me at home while they partied and had their fun was something that I was very used to, but this was not the worst thing that I would become used to. That horrific, familiar act would be molestation. There was a family friend that lived with us, who we'll call "Uncle". Although he was mentally challenged, he was very helpful around the house and helped us whenever we needed it. Naturally, when my parents went out, he babysat me. While they were out doing their thing, Uncle was doing his own thing with me. He would force me to fondle him in ways that I had no clue about. After a couple of incidences with him, I told my mom. She was shocked and did not want to believe me. For her, Uncle was her meal ticket; he supplied her with cigarettes and gas money. Now, could cigarettes and gas money possibly be more important than a mother protecting her four year old from a pedophile? She asked me if I was sure, and then she confronted him. He left for a couple of weeks and then started coming back around. When he was allowed to move back in, I quickly learned my worth. What could I do if my own mother did not believe me or allow me to have security in my own home? Who would defend me?

It was at this time that I began to dissociate. For those of you who may not be familiar with dissociative identity disorder, it is more commonly known as multiple personality disorder. We'll dig into this disorder little more later on. But for the sake of this point in my life, I will just express that multiple personality disorder was my only defense mechanism. I literally split into different people, and my behavior began to change drastically in an attempt to preserve my sanity. I recall times when I would wear several pairs of underwear at once. In my mind, this was the only logical way for me to protect myself. One day, while I was preparing for my bath, my mom asked me why I had so many pairs of underwear on. Of course would not answer. I mean why would I tell her when she didn't believe me in the first place? By allowing him to move back in, Uncle was given a free pass to do whatever he wanted to do to me. Instead of making me fondle him, he had reversed the roles and was now touching me. Although there were supposedly conditions under which he was allowed to re-enter our home, those ground rules meant absolutely nothing to me. Clearly there were no boundaries, and there certainly was no justice for me. I had no one to fight for me or defend me. After everything I told my mom, my parents *still* left me with him. I couldn't trust anyone, not Mom not Dad, NO ONE! The molestation continued off and on until I was about 13. In the meantime, the alcohol abuse, drug addiction, and domestic violence continued between my parents.

Stripped of Innocence

Have you ever felt like you were born with a bull's eye on your forehead? Have you ever questioned why certain things repeatedly happened to you? I was convinced that I was targeted for sexual abuse and sexually explicit behavior. After all, it was permitted in my home with no consequence. There were seeds that the enemy planted in my life from very early on, and he continuously sent agents to water those seeds. A vicious cycle had begun in my mind, which began to control my thoughts and actions moving forward.

One summer, I stayed with my aunt and her two girls in an effort to try to escape from reality and partake in a place of refuge. I enjoyed visiting with my cousins, but this home proved to be another harsh reminder of the abandonment and rejection that was hovering over me like a dark, black cloud. My aunt was a heroin addict and like my home I was left to fend for myself and my two cousins. . On this particular day while she left us, I remember having to cook hamburgers for us to eat. My aunt had neglected to even think about how or what we would do when we got hungry. She also had not cared as to what her children and I were or would do while she was gone. They had a next door neighbor, who was African American. He was just a couple years older than I was and my cousins let him in the back door like they had many times. They introduced me to him as one of their friends. I was cautious as to this stranger but again there was nothing I could do. At one point, we were left alone and he tried to kiss me. Me sternly saying 'no" meant nothing as he pushed me down on the floor and forced himself on me. He raped me and left as casually as someone who had just finished using the bathroom and zipping up their pants. I didn't tell anyone in the house about what happened, as I asked myself, "What was the point?" I had no voice, and my feelings didn't matter to anyone up to this point. I called my mom, hoping that she would come and get me. She responded with an attitude that was just as casual and nonchalant as the boy who raped me. "You'll be fine." In fact, she didn't come and get me until two days later. So here I was again, left to fend for myself. Enduring such hardness and neglect just left me not even caring about myself. No one cared about me so why should I care for myself.

The level of dissociation began to increase drastically, to the point where I began to black out. I would literally forget large intervals of time and was unable to recall what I said or did. Hatred and mistrust built up and I began to act out in school and engaged in sexually explicit behavior. I 'played house' with my neighbors all the time because my mother always threw me off on other people. She never nurtured me and was not able to connect with me. As I look back, I understand that she was only doing what she knew how to do because of how she had been raised. I have since forgiven her and have been blessed to be a good mother to my own children as a way to stop the trend.

But at this particular time in my life expressed here, I was constantly getting into fights and repeating the cycle of abuse that I grew up with at home. I learned how to be deceitful and cunning. I simply did not care about anyone, including myself, anymore. I bartered cigarettes, a ride, money, or whatever I wanted to Uncle in exchange for what he wanted. This was easy because Uncle was still living with us. At this time, in the third grade, I was now smoking cigarettes. So, I sold my body and would let him fondle me and perform oral sex on me to get these cigarettes or other things I needed. The enemy had me trapped in a downward spiral designed to take me out.

Looking for Love in All the Wrong Places

All the emotional pain that I had experienced up to this point was enough to make anyone lose their sanity completely. Among all the forced sexual nightmares upon me, I also experienced multiple sexual encounters with men who were married into my family. Sex made me feel love. It was the only way I could feel like I mattered or like I had any worth at all. The attention that I needed was found when I gave my body away.

I got my first meaningful attention when I was thirteen, and I met Peter. His grandparents lived next door to my cousin's house, and he had come from Florida to spend the summer with them. He came to my cousin's graduation party and we talked to each other for the first time. Although there was a significant age difference, we got along just fine. He was nineteen, and his interest in me made me believe that he loved me. That night, we went downstairs into the basement started making out and then had intercourse. Against my dad's wishes, he and I officially became boyfriend and girlfriend. Mom allowed me to see him in spite of all of Dad's protests. I would barter my way out of being grounded so that Peter and I could see each other.

There were always parties going on in my house, and alcohol and drug abuse reigned. During these parties, I would steal cigarettes while the adults weren't looking. One night, I got a hold of a pack of cigarettes that had joints inside. I decided to take them and save them to try later. The next day, my younger brother Chris and I decided to walk a couple of miles to meet a friend. I smoked the joint and made him smoke it too, so he wouldn't tell on me. I refused to be the only one to go down if we were to get caught. As I began to feel the effects of it, I began to hallucinate. It looked like pieces of concrete were falling from the overpass as we walked by it. I was terrified and tried to make Chris stop smoking it, but he refused. This was my first experience with marijuana, but Chris later told me that he had tried it before. When we finally met up with our friend, I was extremely dehydrated and needed water badly, so we stopped at a house where an elderly couple lived. We knocked on the door and asked for a cup of water, and met a lady who was actually so sweet to us. Somehow, I had sprained my ankle and couldn't walk any further. She tried to call my mom, but I had taken the phone off the hook before I left the house so that my parents could sleep. Just then, we saw Uncle driving down the road, so I ran out to the road and motioned for him to stop. He took us home and I slept until the next day where I woke up to Dad questioning me about his missing joint. I denied that I knew anything about it, and he flew into a rage. Apparently, there was something added to those joints; in other terms they were laced with *something.* Not only did I hallucinate, but I slept for almost an entire day. These simple red flags were enough to alert my dad of me being the primary suspect. He threatened to beat me, cussed at me, and said all types of degrading and humiliating things to me. When he left, I gave the cigarette pack to my brother and he tossed it outside. He called Dad and asked, "Is this what you're looking for?" Chris took the fault, Dad took the pack to get his fix, and I took whatever pieces of my heart were still left and walked away.

Now back to Peter. In the midst of all the continued experiments and turmoil at my house, Peter and I were still seeing each other. I would meet him at the gate located at the end of our property. He would pick me up and we'd go park somewhere, drink, and spend time together. Nothing else seemed to matter, as I felt that life was perfect in my own little world with just him and me. My time with Peter was time well spent. I didn't have to worry about the violence between Mom and Dad or the craziness with Uncle. Peter loved me and I loved him. No one could convince me otherwise. He rescued me from all the craze in my life, and I was determined that we were going to be together forever.

During one of our 'getaways', Peter took me to an apartment in an abandoned building. We spent the entire weekend there together while we drank and smoked. When he dropped me off at the gate on Monday, Dad was waiting there to ground me. He had found out from Mom that I had been with Peter. While Peter and I were away, there was no place for us to wash ourselves. I had developed a genital rash from not bathing, and I went to show it to Mom, as any daughter should be able to. This will show you just how emotionally distant and out of touch Mom was when it came to me, as she sent me to my dad so that he could take a look at it. He explained to me that it was not an STD, but that it was caused by the lack of hygiene during my escapade with Peter. This led to Mom and Dad having a huge fight, and forbidding me from having any communication with Peter. I still did what I had to do to talk to him, even if it meant splitting the telephone line and connecting it to the line underneath the house regularly. I also had opportunities to see him when I went outside to check the mail. Our summer romance would soon come to an end because it was time for Peter to leave and go back to Florida. I was determined that nothing was going to keep us apart, and there was no one who could stop us from being together. So when Peter had to leave, I was ready to leave too and run away.

Life as Runaway

The idea of not being with Peter was unbearable. I could not stand the thought of being away from him. He protected me and made me feel safe like no one else ever had in my life. When we were together, I felt like I was the most special thing in the world. Peter had a bus ticket to return home, but I didn't. So as any couple would do we decided to stay together, even if it meant to hitch-hike. With a small bag of clothes in hand and Peter's name written all over my heart, I was ready. We hopped on a freight train headed for Ohio and then hitched a ride with a truck driver for the next hour. With no money or a place to sleep, we slept in a cornfield overnight, and had ramen noodles for dinner. The next morning, we found a creek and bathed in it. As we walked to the interstate to hitch another ride, a state trooper picked us up and took us to the patrol office. The officer questioned Peter, and ultimately I was taken to a foster home. Life as I knew it was over. I did get to go to a home with a very warm and welcoming couple. This was new to me, and they actually made me something to eat. Their hospitality was great, but in my mind, I was trying to cook up a way to run away again. I wondered what happened to Peter and I had to find some way to get to Florida so I could be with him again.

After a short stay in foster care, Mom and one of our cousins came to get me. Mom cussed and fussed and expressed just how angry she was with me. If anyone had a right to be angry, I was the one who held that right. I was tired of the fighting and drama at home. I was sick of Uncle messing with me.

I tried to tell Mom how much I loved Peter and that I wanted to be with him. Her response was basically in the neighborhood of, "If you want Peter than I am done with you."

The ride was very uncomfortable, to put it nicely, as we drove back to Indiana, Only God knows what I would have to deal with once I got home. While riding we passed a truck stop where I saw none other than Peter! I begged my mom to stop and pick him up, and she obliged. He was her means of getting me off her hands. She went through the 'parental motions' of cussing him out and telling him about how wrong he was to take me away. As she went on, I danced inside because Peter and I were together again. While Mom and my cousin were talking, he and I had sex in the back seat. They were clueless. My hero was back in my arms, and nothing or no one else mattered. My place of safety and security was with Peter, whether we were in an abandoned building, heading to Florida, or in the back seat of a car going back to Indiana. When we arrived in Indiana, Mom dropped him off to his grandmother's, and then took me home. Peter then left for Florida and somehow, I convinced my mom to let me go too so I could be with him. She agreed to let me go only if Peter's mom would make sure that I went to school. She promised Mom that she would and I was off for Florida again. Since Peter had already been sent back, I had to travel alone this time. But, Peter bought my bus ticket so it wouldn't be so bad. I had left Indiana to live with him in Florida for what would become the next seven months.

Reality Sets In

I was on top of the world; I could not get to Peter fast enough. When I got to Florida, he was in an inpatient treatment facility for alcoholics. While he stayed there, I was at his home with his mother and younger brother, Marcus. Marcus and I shared a room and began to become better acquainted with each other. I really missed Peter while he wasn't there and I craved attention. Marcus and I kissed one time; and that one time we did, to our shock, Peter came through the window! I completely freaked out. His mom was very distraught when she discovered that he was home and did not complete the treatment program.

Despite the agreement Peter's mother made with Mom, I never went to school, and no one made me. During the day, while Marcus went to school, I stayed home, watched television, and relaxed by the pool. Peter's mother never pressured me about anything and was very cordial toward me. She had her own legal issues to deal with, and she actually had to serve time in jail for a previous offence. When Peter's mother went to jail all of our lives were suddenly shifted. Peter's dad returned to the house to take care of Marcus, while Peter and I went to live with his older brother. Living with Peter's older brother didn't last very long because their relationship was very volatile. They just could not get along. We ended up leaving, and with no place to go, we wound up staying and sleeping in the woods. We eventually found an abandoned house we could use for shelter, and made ourselves comfortable there. At this point, I was used to 'roughing it.' I had learned how to survive, not only emotionally, but physically away from the norm. We stayed in that house for a couple of days, eating only snacks and drinks from the local gas station. This was certainly no walk in the park. During our tenure in that abandoned house, we had no way to bathe and no warm meals. Bouncing from place to place was not what I had in mind when I begged my mom to let me come to stay with Peter, but for love, I was willing to do just about anything.

Peter was finally able to get a hold of a friend of his who was willing to let us stay with him for a few days. With Peter's friend, we at least got to sleep on a hideaway couch. Mentally, I was in about to be in a world of confusion. All that mattered is that I had Peter. His attention filled the places of emptiness in my heart. That same attention, along with the love, nurture, and validation that I couldn't find from anyone else, he provided. At least on the surface that's the way it seemed. What transpired next just took me further down the path of destruction that the enemy had assigned to my life to destroy my self-worth and literally take what was left of hope I had in my mind.

One day, Peter forced me to have sex with him while his friend watched. To make matters worse, this guy's house was filled with pornographic tapes. So for all I knew, I could have become part of a repetitive act that took place in that home and we could have been recorded. I didn't want to do it, but he forced himself on me. This dream of starting my life over with Peter in Florida had quickly turned into a hellish nightmare. What in the world did I get myself into? The person I thought loved me had now become just like everyone else. . At this point, reality began to sink in, as I was in serious trouble again. Although I didn't want to believe this was happening, I feared for my safety even with Peter by my side. From trap houses, to abandoned buildings, to sleeping in corn fields, I had given all I could to Peter, and this was how he treated me. This was not the person that I fell in love with. This was just another person who was beginning to disappoint me in my life.

Trapped

Knowing that I really didn't have any other option at this time, Peter and I moved back to his house and lived with his dad and brother while his mom was still away in prison serving time. While we stayed there, Peter got a job stocking shelves at a local Winn Dixie. With him working, we saved up enough money to rent a house. On the one hand, I was happy because we had our own place and could be alone. On the other hand, I was alone and very isolated from the world. I did not know anyone, but it wouldn't matter if I did, because I was not allowed to leave the house. While Peter worked I was home alone, washing his clothes, keeping the house in order, and doing other things trying to be 'domestic.' Just that quickly, I became a victim of domestic abuse. I couldn't believe how quickly the tables had turned.

Later on, I learned that Peter was a paranoid schizophrenic. Not only was I trapped in the house, but I could not open any curtains or doors. One day I attempted to mail my mom a letter and when he found out, he attacked me. He beat me in the head. When I tried to run out of the house, he chased me and choked me to the point that I almost blacked out. I was stunned, hurt, and of course scared. As a typical batterer would do, he apologized to me and said that he didn't mean to do it. He vowed to never hit me again. I accepted his apology, trying to be optimistic about Peter and I's future. Things were good for a while, but of course, the abuse continued. I recall one incident in particular where he was very angry. I don't remember what triggered his mood; but he forced himself on me and took out his box cutter, threatening to cut up my face if I left him. He said no one would want me, so I accepted that and let him have his way.

As time went on, things went from bad to worse in Peter's care. I came to the realization that I wasn't Peter's girlfriend, but rather his prisoner. The only people I was allowed to converse with were the married couple that he rode with to work. I had their telephone number in case of emergency, but I never used it. Eventually, Peter lost his job, leading to us losing the house. Of course, we ended up moving back in with his dad.

Peter's mental challenges caused him to act very irrationally and unreasonably. Although we had the shelter of the house, he decided to build a campfire and make us stay in the woods behind his house. One night he began to ask me questions about his brother and what went on between us. I panicked and wondered why he was bringing this up now. I knew he was going to hit me, so I pretended that I had to use the bathroom. When I got far enough away, I took off running to the neighbor's house. She was a police officer, and I told her everything that was going on with Peter. I then asked her to help me get back to Indiana. I explained to her that I was afraid that he would beat me again. She called my mom, and they worked to get me a bus ticket home. The only problem was that I could not leave until the following day.

The officer took me to Peter's co-worker and his wife's house. However, his wife was not home. Instead he had some guests over that night while he was watching their two year old son. When I arrived, they were all watching sports on TV. Naturally, he let me in, and I sat down and watched sports with them. The only thing on my mind was getting away from Peter and getting back to Indiana in one piece. It was pathetic that this was my only concern in a house full of people having fun and spending time as friends. One of the men there began to flirt with me, so I decided to go to my safe place, the bathroom. As I proceeded to leave the bathroom, he was standing in the doorway. As I attempted to pass him, he grabbed me and tried to kiss me. I refused, got away, and went back to the living room. I fell asleep on the couch and the houseguests soon left.

At some point, Peter's co-worker's wife came home; but as she so often did, left the door to the house unlocked. Everyone was sleeping, and the next thing I knew, I was awakened by Peter's hand over my mouth. Needless to say, I freaked out. Again I told him that I had to use

the bathroom. On my way, I ran into the bedroom, jumped on the bed, and woke Peter's co-worker up. I was frantic. He got up and went out into the living room to talk to Peter while I stayed in the room with his wife. He confronted him about trespassing and threatened to call the police if he didn't leave. He told him that I was going back to Indiana, and with that, Peter left.

The next day, Peter's co-worker and his wife dropped me off at the bus station. I used a pay phone to call my mom and let her know that I was coming home. Suddenly, a sheriff pulled up and asked me where I was going. He took me to the sheriff's station and called my mom, asking her why I was traveling alone. He then questioned me and I told him that I was a runaway. He confirmed the story with Mom and put me on the bus back to Indiana. This entire time, Peter was calling my mom, threatening to come back to Indiana. He told her that he was going to set our house on fire and kill us all.

When Mom picked me up from the bus station, she told me what was happening with Peter. She told me that he was on his way back to Indiana. A couple days later, he was there. I was terrified more than ever before. Peter was very acquainted with the woods and had no problem doing whatever he had to do to carry out his plans. I was constantly in fear because I didn't know if he was hiding in the woods behind my house, or when he might suddenly pop up. He still called every day and threatened us. I wanted to come home and here I was, but I was still trapped.

There's No Place Like Home?

It would have been nice to have some sense of relief or comfort when I returned back home to Indiana, but I didn't. There was no such thing as 'home sweet home' for me upon my return. My family was torn apart. I mentioned earlier that Mom and Dad would eventually get divorced, and this very horribly placed time was where that life event also fit in. I overheard Dad talking on the phone to a woman he had agreed to go live with in Alabama. I wanted to go with him, but he said that I couldn't because I wasn't his child. Dad did take my younger brother and sister (his biological children, Tiffany and Chris) and moved to Alabama. My mom stripped my dad of everything he had and once again, I was crushed. The only father-figure that I knew was gone. My self-worth, sense of belonging, and protection were all burned to ash, as they had been before. Mom started dating another man, who was another alcoholic. I began to self-medicate to try and ease the pain I was feeling. I drank alcohol and I smoked marijuana. As long as I was numb and couldn't feel anything, I could manage.

Meanwhile, Mom and her new beau, Greg, lived in the bar. Mom and I moved into an apartment near the factory where she worked and Greg moved in with us. Nothing had changed. Mom would go directly to the bar from work so that she and Greg could drink the night away. She enrolled me in school and I went whenever I felt like it, and that wasn't very often. The dynamics of life at home were like a volcano waiting to explode. For years, I had held in so much hurt, frustration, anger, disappointment, and bitterness against my mother. On this one evening Mom decided to actually be home, everything suddenly came to a head. For the first time, I physically attacked my mom and cussed at her. I had finally come to the point where I could no longer pretend that everything was okay. We fought until Greg pulled us apart and Mom locked herself in the bathroom and took a handful of pills. Before she could go through with it, Greg made her open up the door and forced her to spit them out.

Feeling like less of a family than ever before, I went to stay with Mom's brother, Richard and his two sons, Marshall and Mackey. I enjoyed spending time with my cousins. Marshall and I were the same age, and the three of us went to school together. We also all drank and smoked together. This was my relief from the hell of being at home. I went back and forth between houses. Ultimately being home caused me to relive the nightmare of domestic violence, as Mom and Greg constantly fought.

In the meantime, Peter found out from the local grocer where we now lived. One night, very late, I woke up to the sound of tapping on my window. When I went to see what was causing the noise, I saw him standing outside. I immediately woke my mom up and let her know that he was outside. Mom and Greg let him come in from the cold. He apologized for everything he had done and went on to explain to us that he had been staying at a nearby church for a couple of days, sleeping under the pulpit. This particular church kept their doors unlocked so that people could come in at any time to pray. I fell for his story and let him stay with us for a couple of days. As I recalled, sex appeased him and kept him calm. It also kept him from beating me, so we were intimate. The next day, he was gone, never to be seen again.

The Cycle Continues

As if life couldn't get any worse, Mom sent me to live with my biological dad's brother, Uncle Samuel, and his family. Uncle Samuel was married and had four sons of his own. All of Uncle Sam's boys were older than me except one, who was my age. She claimed that I needed help and that she could not live with me. Apparently Uncle Samuel's family atmosphere was the right answer for me in her eyes. I hated her and blamed her for how horrible my life had become. Uncle Sam was strict, but I was glad to get away from my mother. After all, maybe this new situation would get me back on track. Just then did I discover that Uncle Sam was a binge drinker, as he drank constantly for months at a time without eating. He would pass out at night and then get up and start the cycle all over again. It just so happened that I moved in during one of his drinking spells, and he and my aunt were having an argument over how the two younger boys should be disciplined. Violence suddenly erupted. My thought was, 'Here we go again'. In spite of this, I was still glad to be away from home.

My aunt was very loving toward me and was a breath of fresh air in my cloudy life. Things were going good with them until one night my aunt and uncle discovered me sleepwalking with a pair of scissors in my hand. Apparently, I was making a motion as though I was going to stab myself. They conversed with Mom and then began to seek out psychiatric help for me. He was very concerned about my well-being and was adamant about me getting help. He was *not* happy with the way Mom had raised me and handled certain situations. The fact that she would allow me to run off with a nineteen year old was beyond him. It made me feel loved and wanted to be with my uncle and aunt.

A Glimmer of Hope

Auntie and Uncle Sam made an appointment for me to visit a psychiatrist named Dr. Frederick. He engaged me in talk therapy, and it proved to be very helpful. There was so much bottled up inside of me that I needed to release. In addition to talk therapy, Dr. Frederick placed me on antidepressants. While I was on the meds, I had a terrible nightmare about my siblings being taken away from me. The nightmare made me fight in my sleep, to the point that I gave myself a bloody nose. I continued with the talk therapy and kept a journal on the side when I wasn't talking with Dr. Frederick. I was able to release my feelings and express myself freely by both talking to a professional and writing on my own. Finally, I was beginning to feel hope. I was not drinking or using any marijuana at all. I did not want to go back home and to my surprise, Uncle Sam allowed me to stay.

During this time, I attended school, but I had to be retained because I had missed so much school back home. One day, I decided to hang out after school and smoke cigarettes with friends. For this, I was grounded for two weeks. I was not used to the grounding that my aunt and uncle placed me on. I had to do chores, eat, and then go to bed, period. After I endured enough of being 'locked down', I decided to sneak out of my bedroom window one evening and go to a friend's house. Uncle Sam came right behind me and escorted me right back into the house. He added an additional week to my punishment. The punishment sucked, but at least it made me realize that someone actually cared about me.

When Easter arrived, Mom came to visit me and took me shopping. It was nice to see her and spend some time with her. I usually didn't wear dresses, but I wanted to buy a dress so that I could dress up. I *never* wore dresses, so this again was something new to me. During her visit, I asked my mom if I could stay with my friend Tracy for the rest of the school year and summer. Tracy lived with her mother and grandmother, who were also much stricter than I was used to. Mom, Uncle Sam, and my aunt consented, coming to the agreement that after the summer I would return back home to live with her and Greg. Although Tracy's mom was strict, I still had a little leeway after school. I didn't have to come straight home like I did with my aunt and uncle. I still kept up with the therapy, but I decided that I didn't want to take the meds anymore. So, I just quit cold turkey.

During my summer stay at Tracy's house, I met a young African American guy named Wayne. Wayne and I would meet and he'd give me pot to smoke. I enjoyed my summer not only because I was free from Uncle Sam's 'iron rule,' but because I met new friends through my enrollment in school and through Wayne. Soon, my summer fun had ended and I had to move back with Mom. I was moving back in with my mom for what seemed like the hundredth time, and I was doing it just in time to turn sixteen.

Caught Up In a Whirlwind

When I arrived home Mom and Greg were still together, but she was also still in the process of divorcing Paul. I went to school and eventually got caught up in the same madness that I thought I had escaped when I went to stay with Uncle Sam. I hung out with my cousins, and again we became a very close-knit bunch. We smoked, drank, and listened to music together all the time. Marijuana was always so readily available and I took advantage. In school, I had a friend named Mark who was very flashy and flamboyant in his mannerisms. Other people labeled him 'gay', but he was a very good friend to me. In my eyes, he was just a friend who acted like a girl. He introduced me to his brother, Adam, and shortly after, Adam and I became an item.

In contrast to what I was accustomed to, Adam was a true gentleman. He was very compassionate towards me and treated me with so much care. Contrary to my relationship with Peter, Adam was my very first true love. He was never violent and always showed me respect. But, he was an alcoholic and smoked a lot. This was the point in my life where I began to experiment with prescription drugs while hanging out with Mark. I also drank straight hard liquor and whiskey instead of just beer. I couldn't handle beer because it left me unable to function, but I was fine with the hard stuff.

By this time Mom and Dad's divorce was final, and she was getting custody of Tiffany and Chris. This was exciting for Mom and me. My happiness didn't last long as Mom started putting them off on me so that she and Greg could go live it up and drink the night away at the bar. To add to the chaos, Mom and Greg got married without me knowing. While I was staying with some friends, they had a preacher come to a hotel room and marry them. Greg's son and Tiffany were the only ones in attendance. I didn't care that I wasn't there because I didn't want any part of it anyway. I stayed away from home as much as possible and Mom didn't seem to really even notice. Most of my time was spent with my cousins, friends, and Adam.

I Hurt, You Hurt

I was constantly getting into fights at school, I mean *constantly.* I had no sense of direction in my life and there was certainly no guidance for me. Once, I was given an in-school suspension for three days for fighting on the school bus. On another occasion, I got into a fight and was sent to the principal's office. I refused to be paddled so the school called my mom to come and get me. Subsequently, I had to be signed out of school completely. My principal was gracious enough to allow me to attend summer school to try and make up for some of my lost time. However, on the last day of school, I had a fight with a girl who kept talking about me. I banged her head against a locker and on the floor. Again, I ended up in the principal's office. As far as I was concerned, there was nothing to talk about. Adam's cousin Kirk walked in the office and offered me a ride, so I left without seeing the principal and without finishing summer school. I was officially a drop-out, and I didn't care one bit.

One night while I was at home and not at school, Adam came over. He had just left a concert, and stopped by just so we could have sex. A few days later, I began to experience terrible itching and irritation in my private area. When I went to investigate and see what was causing it, I saw tiny black specks. I began to try and pull them off of me, when they began to crawl! I lost it. I completely freaked out. What *was* this? What did Adam give me? In a desperate attempt to get relief, I sprayed hair spray on the area, applied rubbing alcohol, and shaved. When I told Mom, she confirmed that it sounded like I had crabs. Her exact response was, "Oh, well." To make matters worse, when I told her what I had done to try and remove them, she laughed hysterically.

I immediately called Adam and confronted him. Without hesitation he denied that I had acquired this mess from him. "I must have gotten them from the port-a-potty at the concert" was his best response to the situation. I didn't believe him and decided to talk to his brother Mark about it. I knew that I could confide in Mark; he was my best friend. He told me what could have been the worst news at the time, which was that his brother was lying about the situation. How could Adam betray me? I just *knew* he was cheating, but I couldn't prove it. I couldn't put my hand on what the problem was, but things had become very different between us. He stopped coming around as much as he had previously done, and he started standing me up when we were supposed to hangout. The anger inside me grew and grew, to the point that I became very confrontational and physically abusive toward him. I started hanging out and drinking with his friends, and I treated him very mean and cold when I did see him. In my eyes it was only fair that he feel what I was feeling. Eventually, Adam's mom placed him in an inpatient program for addicts and asked me to join him so that we could get help together. I started living with him and agreed to go. At the advice of his mother, I started attending Al anon meetings. But I refused to admit that I was an addict. She also encouraged me to go back to school to get my CNA certification, so I did. With the certification, I started working at a nursing home. I didn't have much time to enjoy my new job because as soon as I got it, I lost it. Partying and getting drunk were more important to me than making money and trying to straighten out my life.

While Adam was away in treatment, I partied with our friends and enjoyed myself to the fullest. My nights consistently involved getting high and having fun. One night, Miles, a mutual friend of Adam and mine, had a house party. Kirk and I went to the party together. At the part I became so intoxicated that I had to lie down. A few minutes later, I woke up to someone crawling on top of me and starting to kiss me. It was Miles, I quickly pushed him away. He *knew* that I was dating Adam, and thought that maybe I had enough hatred to betray Adam. Even though he served me a raw deal, I still remained loyal to him. Miles left me alone and didn't bother me again.

Adam remained in treatment for about two months. I wish he would have stayed longer because after he returned home he relapsed and went right back to partying and drinking. At this point, I was told that I had gotten the crabs from him because he was cheating on me. My suspicions were confirmed, and I was determined to get him back for the heartbreak and embarrassment he had caused me. Out for revenge, I went to a party one night at our friends. While partying, Adam had passed out and I had the perfect chance to sleep with his friend, Jason. So I did, and Adam had no idea what had happened until the next heated argument we got in and I told him. We broke up, and I left to again go back home to my mom. Eventually, we reconciled, but our relationship was extremely volatile and violent this time around. I was so aggressive toward him. As I look back on it now, he was stuck paying for all I had endured way before I ever met him. Whenever we would have disagreements, things would escalate to a level of physical violence. For this reason, he would always try to avoid fighting with me. A lack of communication and constant agony for two years, led us to breaking up again. This time, it was for good.

Near Death

After Adam and I broke up, I started dating Kirk. I stayed with him, his dad, and his brother quite often. This one particular night, when Kirk and I had an argument, altered the course of the rest of my life. I wanted to go home and he refused to take me because the weather was very bad. He went to bed and I slept on the couch. Later, he apologized and proceeded to make sexual advances on me. I refused him. He didn't care as he held my hands over my head, forced himself on me and raped me. I just cried myself to sleep like I had done so many times. The next day, he finally took me home, and he went to school.

By now, I'm sure that you've gathered that partying was my life. It was my escape from all the hell I was living in. There was nothing else that seemed to soothe my pain like getting drunk or high. So naturally that is what I did after the incident with Kirk. Also like you have gathered up to this point, I forgive people, and most of the time it is too soon or too easily. So naturally, a couple weeks later, Kirk had a party at his house that I attend. There was tons of alcohol and crushed pills that they snorted and smoked, but on this particular night I only drank. One of Kirk's friends, Kyle, was at the party. Kyle just lived right down the street so he had left his car in the driveway and walked to the party. We decided to drive it to him, so me, Kirk, and his friend Trent went and got the car. Trent was completely intoxicated and decided to take the car around the block for a spin.

Kirk got in, and we headed down the road. Just then, Trent crossed over the highway and drove down the country road. He started to speed, and Kirk encouraged him to do so. Alcohol, narcotics, and impaired mental capacities created an atmosphere ripe for the enemy to snatch our souls away for all eternity. I saw that Trent had a glaze over his eyes, and I knew we were in trouble. Something awful was about to happen, and I could sense it. Suddenly, we hit a metal pole, as my face simultaneously hit the windshield of the car. I heard Trent gurgling, struggling for air, and Kirk was unconscious. Somehow, I managed to get out of the car. I tried to walk but could not at all. I could feel that there were bones in my body that were crushed. I struggled to crawl to a house that had a security light on it about a quarter of a mile away. I knocked on the door, awaiting the arrival of a farmer who answered. He seemed hesitant to help me at first, but after I told him that my friends were dying, he immediately called the paramedics. Upon examination, my vertebrae and pelvis were fractured, and I had glass embedded in the side of my neck and head. Kirk and Trent were not as badly injured as I was, or as bad as I had thought they were. Trent had bruised ribs and Kirk walked away with only a few cuts and bruises. I had to remain in the hospital for several days following the accident. When Kirk told Miles about the accident and my injuries, he acted as if the situation was not severe at all. Miles, standing up for me and faulting Kirk and Trent, was not happy about it at all. God *had* to be with me that night, or else I probably would not have been alive.

Rehab/12 Steps... Backward

When I was released from the hospital, I was prescribed very heavy meds. My mobility was limited, and I could not get up and down the steps, nor would the doctor let me. I was pretty much confined to the couch and living- room. In an effort to try and take care of me and actually act like a parent, Mom bought me a puppy named Gizmo. He was great company while he was with me. However my enjoyment was short-lived, as Gizmo died of parvovirus a short while later. At this point, Kirk served absolutely no purpose to me, so we broke up. I made frequent trips to the doctor for refills of my pain meds. He warned me that the pills were narcotic and potentially addictive, but being the rebellious person that I was I just took them whenever I wanted. I had gotten addicted to them. I was absolutely out of control, even more so than before. You would have thought that the car accident would have been enough to jolt me into reality, but it wasn't. I stole money from my mother to buy marijuana. I spent a lot of time with my brother Chris, his friend Jake, my step-brother William, and his cousin Henry. To show you how much of a wreck my mindset was, let me share this incident with you. One day, Henry decided to write a check from his dad's checkbook and cash it to buy marijuana. Then next time we ran out, it was my turn to write one. So, without hesitation I got my mom's checkbook and wrote one. One night a couple months later, Mom and Greg were at the bar when they bumped into Henry's dad. He told Greg that money had been taken out of his account. He went on to say that he immediately knew, by the handwriting, that it was Henry and I who had written the checks.

When they arrived home from the bar, Greg came at me while I was lying down on the couch. He was cursing and swearing at me like I had never heard him before. I tried to get away from him, and he began to swing at me and hit me right in the face. Needless to say, he was drunk, even thought that is no excuse to hit a young woman. Finally Mom got between us to block the hits, but I pushed her into him and ran out the door. He chased me, pushed me down on the ground, and started kicking me. My mom disrupted him again, and I ran into the house and called my brother Chris. I told him and Jake to meet me near the house on Horse Road. As I was headed out the door, Greg started to come after me again. I took off running into the field as he chased me down to meet Chris and Jake where we had planned on meeting. I went with Jake to his grandmother's house, trying to get a sense of security.

At this point in my life, I had become a professional thief, and I was battling hard core addiction. I was addicted to pills, and I knew I needed help. I finally realized that pretending that nothing was wrong was not going to help me to get any better. I certainly could not wait on anyone else to come and rescue me, as I had been let down so many times. I began to call around in search of a treatment center. Upon finding one, I checked myself into an inpatient program where I stayed for 60 days. All the things Adam's mom taught me about addiction ended up being very helpful at this time. I participated in a 12- step program, and it was here that I learned about a 'higher power'. I was told in the program that I needed a 'higher power' because I was an addict and was helpless. Of course, live I had done so many times; I believed what others had to say.

I took my prescription meds with me into the program, but they were taken away upon arrival. I was only allowed to take Tylenol at the treatment center. The withdrawals I experienced were treacherous and took a toll on me mentally, emotionally, and physically. I had very vivid and strange dreams. In addition, I felt so depleted and drained. I was given plenty of juices to drink and supplements to take. Nutrient rich foods helped in the cleaning process. There were counseling sessions where I was able to release a lot of what I had been holding in for so long about my childhood. We also discussed my relationship with my mom in these sessions. I made friends with a fellow inpatient named Byron. However, at this point, I was not interested in a relationship, AT ALL.

Finally, Family and Friends Day was to be held at the treatment facility. This was an opportunity for me to see my family. In spite of all I had gone through, I still wanted to see them and move forward with my life, hopefully in a positive and different direction. Mom, Greg, William, Chris and Tiffany all came to visit me on this special day. Unfortunately, but not surprisingly, Mom was not engaged in the visit. There were activities designed to counsel the family and help to bring everyone together, but she refused to participate. She never took ownership or responsibility for her role in my upbringing or misdirection. The visit was a complete waste of time for her, and as a result, for me.

My counselor put a plan of release together for me, ensuring that I continued with treatment and counseling as an outpatient. As part of the treatment plan, I was not allowed to return home with Mom. This was fine with me, as I had been away from my mom for more time than I was actually with her. The only other place I could go at this time was to my Aunt Kerry's house. Kerry was

49

mom's twin and had not been a viable part in my life because she herself was a heroin addict. But, she no longer did heroin, instead she just indulged in marijuana and alcohol. As long as I didn't have to go home with Mom, I could care less whom I was living with. As odd as it seems, the officials at the treatment facility never contacted her or investigated to see if her home was a suitable environment for me to live in while I recovered. At the same time, I never disclosed her lifestyle because I was ready to get out of the facility.

Beauty

God in Action/ A Glimpse of Beauty

I didn't see it at the time, but God was setting me up by allowing me to be placed in Aunt Kerry's care. She had a friend name Kimberly who was a mighty Woman of God. Whenever she visited, she would fuss at Kerry about her lifestyle and try to minister the Love of God to her. I saw God through this woman, and I knew *that* she was sent to nurture me and help me to get away from the negativity and drugs that went on in Aunt Kerry's house. To make things even better, she allowed me stay with her. I was not the only one that Kimberly was trying to help, as there was a young man there boarding with her. She was truly a great woman of faith and would pray and prophesy very often. I saw the Power of God move through her. Whenever we needed food, she would pray that we could be able to have that food to survive. Within minutes of her prayer, someone would come and bless us with food or money to buy the things we needed. It was such a blessing in my very troubled life to witness God in action.

In an effort to meet my post-treatment requirements, I got a sponsor and made sure that I attended my daily meeting faithfully. I was determined to accomplish something, and get back on the right track. There was a guy named Byron who was in treatment with me. He lived close to Kimberly, so we started to go to meetings together. Sadly, he ended up relapsing like so many people have done. Although I would like to say that I separated from him and moved on with my life on a beautiful road to sobriety, the truth is that I relapsed right along with him. This time it was only marijuana that I chose to use, but that's beside the point. The principles that we were taught in treatment groomed us to believe that we had no control. So I justified my behavior because I didn't *buy* the marijuana, but only *used* it when it was around me. I immediately started going downhill again. When Kimberly found out that I started using again, I had to leave her house and go back in with Mom. Rightfully so, Kimberly could not and *would* not tolerate sin in her house. On the plus side of going back home, I never communicated with Byron again.

By this time, William, Greg's son, had moved in with Mom and Greg. This meant that I had no bed of my own to sleep in; so I shared a bed with Tiffany. William flirted with me and began to make moves on me regularly. William was only 13, and I was 18. We made out and messed around a few times, but it was not what I wanted. I wanted to party, and I had to get away from him. I had much more fun hanging out with Jake and Miles, so I started to hang out with them again. Miles had come back from Florida and was living in our neighborhood again. When I saw him, he was not the nerdy boy I had remembered from before. He was now much more attractive and very different. I was so impressed with how much he had changed, and I wanted to see more of him. I made a bold step one night and called his mom and asked her to tell Miles that I wanted to go out on a date with him. She told him and before I knew it he called me to set up plans to go out.

The day of our date was…well, let's just say, it was *not* the way I planned to prepare for this date. Earlier that day, Chris, William, and I went biking and decided to do some wheelies on our bikes. All of a sudden, I lost control and crashed. Upon hitting the ground, I lost my front teeth and scratched up my face really bad. I went home and told my mom and got that ever popular response, her laughing right in my face. Miles, not knowing what had happened that day, came to get me anyway. I had no idea how was he going to respond when he saw me toothless and bruised up. I made him promise not to laugh as he arrived at my door and walked me out to the car. When he turned the car light on, he looked at me and smiled, and proceeded to take me out on the date he had promised me. I knew he had to *really* like me to still go out with me after my face had been demolished. We went to his friend's house and smoked and drank. This night, I only had one beer, as I kept telling myself that I had to keep things under control. After what happened at Kimberly's, I knew how far *not* to go. I did not want to go back down that road like I had so many times before. Miles drove me home that night after he had been drinking Once again, God intercepted the plan of the enemy and keep us from ending up in the ditch.

At home, or what had been my home, I didn't have a bed and William was such a nuisance. I had enough of all of it and decided to move in with Jake. Miles and I saw more of each other and began to date. My life slowly began to fall into some semblance of order. At that same time, I got a job at a nursing home and purchased my first car. Those were major accomplishments for me, and gave me a sense of hope. Miles lived with his brother and one of his friends. When I would leave work, I would go straight to Miles' house and hang out for hours. His grandmother lived next door, and she was not fond of the idea of me being there with the 'boys' and hated the idea of me spending night with Miles even more. One morning as I was leaving, I found a note on my car that she had written and left there. In the note she was asking me, "What kind of girl would hang out with a bunch of men." She made it clear that she did not want me staying there late or sleeping over anymore. So, Miles and I decided to come up with a plan to continue to spend nights with each other. Our work schedules conflicted, but we were determined to be together as much as we possibly could. Three weeks after I had received the note on my car, we had saved enough money to get a place of our own. Miles worked two jobs while I worked my job at the nursing home, trying to make things work on our own. Three months later, I was pregnant with our first child.

At Death's Door

After all the chaos and trauma I had gone through in my life, things were beginning to look brighter. It seemed as though I had reached a turning point that was going to take me on a brighter path. Little did I know what I actually would have to go through in order to receive and walk in the new life God had planned for me. Miles and I were expecting a baby, and we were so happy together. I was ready to do whatever it would take to keep moving forward.

My pregnancy was normal. Miles and I enjoyed learning that we were going to have a boy that fall. We went to the hospital on the 23rd of September because I was having contractions. However, we were sent back home because they were not strong enough. The next morning, we returned to the hospital as the contractions just would not stop. After I was examined, the doctor determined that I needed an emergency C-section. Mom and Miles' mom, Mandy, were there with us through the process. Our son, Bryson Lee, was born on September 24, 1991. Because he ingested so much amniotic fluid, he had to be taken to ICU right after he was born. They monitored him very closely while I was trying to recuperate from the cesarean. For some reason, I kept passing blood clots during my recovery after the surgery. Something was very wrong with me. Mom kept saying that something was not right, and she was absolutely correct about that. I was in the fight for my life and didn't even know it at the time.

I was transported by ambulance to another hospital where they induced me into a coma, rather than risking the chance of me slipping into one. The chances of me recovering from a coma would be very slim if I fell into one unassisted. During the eight days that I was in the coma, I died three times. During this time, my body began to fill with fluid. I went from 150 pounds to 225 pounds in those eight days. I was also on a ventilator and dialysis machine the entire time. In addition, my skin had turned orange due to severe jaundice. My family could hardly recognize me at this point. I ended up becoming a guinea pig for a science project that the doctors and medical students were about to take part in. They experimented on me, tried all types of medication, and pumped me full of antibiotics. I was on life support the entire time. As my body continued to deteriorate, the doctors began to lose hope. They called my parents into the room and told them that they had to prepare themselves to pull the plug if I did not come out of the coma within the next couple of days. Doctors also said at that time that I would be a vegetable if I did come out. From what I was told at a later time, there was a tremendous amount of tension in the room. This tension was a direct result of Raymond deciding to come out of the 'woodworks' after being missing for so long and trying to put his input in the matter. Apparently Raymond was trying to make decisions on my behalf. At the same time that I was going through this battle, my baby was also fighting hard to survive. Since Miles and I were not married, Bryson was placed in the temporary custody of my mom. She was responsible for making the proper decisions for him. He stayed in the hospital for five days after he was born, nearly dying three times, but eventually getting to go home with my mother.

I was in very grave condition when Bry finally got to go home. Mom started a prayer line and the family gathered together to pray for me. I had three days to recover before the plug had to be pulled. The time was truly running out on my life. Dad offered to help Mom with Bry so she could stay with me at the hospital. She agreed, and Bry went home with Dad Raymond. The doctors advised Mom to take pictures of Bry and paste them to the machines and equipment around me. They also encouraged her to talk to me, in an extreme effort to try and get me to come out of the coma.

Jesus: True Beauty

Mere words could never adequately describe what I experienced next. If there ever was a lesson that I want you, as the reader, to learn from my testimony, it is this: It does not matter who you are, where you've been, or how low you've fallen. God will give you beauty in exchange for all the ashes that have been created by the enemy. Beauty can rise from what has been burned and destroyed in your life. I learned this first hand when Jesus came to visit me in the hospital.

While I was in the coma, Jesus came and took me to Heaven like he has done to so many other wonderful people. All I can say is that I never imagined that something like this could happen to me, after all the negative things that I have done in my life. We all have heard stories about other people who have had out of body experiences. In contrast, there are other people who may have wondered if such a thing could possibly even be real. Well, I am here to testify that I experienced it firsthand when I was in the cold hospital. My spirit was lifted off that hospital bed, out of my body. I literally saw my body lying down on the bed in the hospital as I was rising up to God's presence. But, I looked nothing like I actually was in the natural. There was no jaundice, swelling, or any sign of sickness at all. I looked perfectly normal except for being connected to the machine that I was hooked up to.

Jesus allowed me to get a small glimpse of the beauty of this wonderful place called Heaven; that He himself has prepared for His people. The colors were so vibrant in Heaven, and the peace was overwhelming. I cannot explain with human words the awe and splendor of what I was experiencing at that time in my life. Heaven was, as we so commonly say, out of this world! In addition to the splendor of Heaven, Jesus also took me to Hell. It was horribly dark in Hell. I mean the darkness was so thick, like when you have your eyes closed, but at that moment I didn't. I could hear people screaming and yelling in torment. The very atmosphere was one of complete horror and hopelessness. I could not see anything, but I could clearly hear blood curdling screams of people being tortured. The spirit of fear was so strong that I felt like I was going to have a heart attack, in my spirit. Just when I felt like I could not stand anymore, I was whisked away.

After this, I had a vision of two 'figures' wrestling. One was a white silhouette body and one was a dark figure. I knew the battle was being fought on my behalf. Jesus was fighting my battle for me. On the third day, so naturally a Sunday, I came out of the coma. Glory to God!

Let the Healing Begin

The doctors were in absolute shock that I had risen from my coma, just in time to rectify my life! As I was waking up from the coma, they called my mom and the rest of the family into the room to see me. Upon waking up, I had no idea where I was. At first, I thought I was still pregnant because I was so swollen from all of the blood clots. I had no recollection of anyone coming to visit me in the hospital. I was very sick still but I was still alive. My family sat down and told me what had transpired over the past couple of weeks. I was so out of it, and I couldn't talk because I was still incubated. I had catheters in my chest and in my groin. At some point, the doctors removed the breathing tube, and it felt like my nose was being ripped off my face.

My family came to the hospital to visit more and more over the next few days. I was so happy to see them each and every time. The only nerve-racking time was   when my sister came to visit with my mom. I frantically told my mom to get her out of my room. She was nine years old and clumsy as could be. I just *knew* that she would knock something over or unplug something that would result in the death of me. I preferred that she stayed in the 'window room' and see me from there.

In the midst of all the wonderful company in the hospital, my family brought Bry in so I could see him for a few minutes. He had to be covered from head to toe to protect him from the germs in the room. Seeing him alive and well was such a blessing. Although I had only been in a coma for eight days, my body went through so much. During my recovery process, I experienced tremendous spiritual warfare and mental attack. When the respiratory therapist would come to administer my treatment, he would always ask me about my baby and how he was doing. I was convinced that he was coming to take my baby from me every time. At night, I would see nurses and aids taking people and hiding them under the stairway. One night, I saw a blue colored head floating in my room; the devil was adamant about tormenting me. His tactics to take my life did not succeed so he had to try something, yet God had a plan to stop all of this mental confusion that was taking place.

I was in ICU for a total of fifteen days and then I was moved to recovery. I had no idea that my Dad had been visiting me at this time. The very day I was being taken to recovery, I asked for my step-dad. As I was on my way to recovery, I saw my dad and step-mom at the end of the hall. I couldn't believe after all these years and all the hurt he had caused me, there he was, standing in the recovery room. My heart was overwhelmed with emotion, even more so than usual. I was immediately taken back to the day I read the letter he wrote to me that explained why he had to leave me. He was there along with his mother. He told me that he had been helping to take care of Bryson and that he loved me and him very much. He also told me he had thanked God for saving me. We cried together as he encouraged me to follow the Lord from that point on. After twenty years, it was as if the wind blew in and began to sweep the ashes of my life away. I knew of my Dad, but because I never spent time with him, this was very new for me. It was also very overwhelming. Nevertheless, I was elated that he was there to support me and my new family.

Of all the people that came to visit me, let's not forget about Miles and his brother Eddie. I was so weak that I could not feed myself so Eddie took the time to help feed me while he was there. Meanwhile, as I back at home, Miles and I lost our apartment and he had moved back in with Eddie. In the meantime, our belongings were in storage in their grandmother's basement. As time went on, I began to heal and all my organs were restored to full health. The doctors ran a complete scan on me and could not find anything wrong anymore. No one could deny that a miracle had taken place. The best they could do in order to try and medically explain what happened on paper, was to diagnose me with a blood infection called sepsis. This possibly occurred due to dirty instruments or unsanitary working conditions, but we never did find out for sure what caused it.

By the time I was discharged from the hospital, I was about to turn twenty. I left with a little jaundice and a few needle scars on my arm. Other than that, I left the hospital with a clean bill of health. I went to live with Mom again and slept on a twin bed in the living room. In spite of all the obstacles I had dealt with living at home with Mom, I was glad to be there, alive, and in one piece. Here I was, having miraculously escaped the enemy's assignment to kill me and my baby. I was a new mom with no prior experience or knowledge of how to care for a baby. It took me a long time to bond with Bry. I could never stop him from crying, but it seemed as if he would stop instantly when Mom held him. I felt rejected, unwanted, and almost like Bry were her child and not mine. I felt so incapable of mothering him, but for once in my life my mom was actually encouraging to me. She told me to take my time in bonding with him, and eventually we were able to bond just fine.

Miles came to visit me regularly. We often discussed getting a place of our own again. I had a lawsuit in the works from the car accident I was in with Kirk and Trent because I sued Trent's insurance company. I was hoping that by now the case would be settled and we could use the money to buy our place. The lawyer assigned to this case had heard that I was about to die in the hospital and rushed to get the case settled. Miles and I were able to buy our first home together, a mobile home, with the settlement money. It was time for us to move forward with our lives and be a family. I told Miles that I wanted a promise ring for my birthday that year. Yes, I told him he had to 'put a ring on it'! I had died three times in the process of having our child, and our baby also died three times in that hospital bed. Miles was blessed to have us both here with him, and it was time for us to do things the right way. Miles gave me a promise ring like I had asked. Since he didn't have a job, we lived off my settlement.

Same devil, Same Tricks

Miles, Bryson, and I were a family, and we set off to start our lives together. I was starting to get adjusted to my new life and trying to learn how to manage our home. At the same time, I was trying to be the best mother I could be. Eventually, the settlement ran out, and we began to have some serious financial challenges. With a baby and a new home, there was a lot of added responsibility and bills. Miles was not working and we needed money quick, fast, and in a hurry. One day, my cousin Marshall's girlfriend Debra came to a cookout we had at our house. I noticed while she was making conversation with me that she had a stash of cash on her. I was curious as to how she had so much money, so I asked her where she worked. She told me that she worked at a bar and that if I wanted her to, she could help me to get a job there. Not knowing what she actually did at the bar, I agreed and went to work with her. When we got there, she went to the back and came back out in a skimpy outfit. She was an exotic dancer. I had a couple of drinks and thought about how much I really needed the money and how I was very capable of doing what she did. Legally, I could not work there because I was not yet twenty-one; but since I agreed to work with her, she helped me get a fake birth certificate.

I began dancing at the bar that very next day, and did so for about a year. It was impossible for me to work without being intoxicated. In fact, most of the girls I worked with were either alcoholics, addicts of some kind, or high on marijuana nightly. I remember one lady that worked at the bar was just doing it to make extra money after a long week working for a law firm. Underneath all the glitz, glamour, and glitter, these women were all just as broken as me.

I met two girls at the bar who invited me to an underground 'swingers club.' One of them was a member of the club and wanted me and my co-workers to come to the club with our boyfriends. As I have always done in the past, I agreed to take Miles and go. The front of the place was a tile store, but it was a 'cesspool of sin' in the back. A special code was required to get in to this club. I had never, *ever* been to a place like that before. Upon walking in, there was naked people everywhere, performing sexual acts on each other. The group I came with stayed close together. In fact, we stayed with our boyfriends, just observing while having a few drinks. The club was a little much for me and I never went back after that. Shortly after this, I ran into an old friend of mine that I used to live with. I invited her to come and stay with Miles, Bry, and I so that we could catch up. While she was visiting, I invited her to have a threesome with Miles and me. In my mind, if I consented to this, Miles would not cheat on me or be inclined to go back to the club.

I Do

I had many issues with insecurity and trust, but Miles and I really did love each other. Although we didn't have a perfect relationship, we had been blessed with a healthy son and decided it was time to get married. We decided to have a double wedding with my cousin Marshall and his girlfriend, Debra. The date was set for December 6, just days after I turned 21. My dad had come back into my life, so naturally he walked me down the aisle. He had become such a great help to Miles and I. He even purchased furniture for our house, including a baby bed for Bry. He later told me that he had made a covenant with God, promising Him that if He would heal Bry and me, that he would dedicate his life completely to Him. God fulfilled His end of the deal, and now Dad was living out his.

A year after the wedding, Miles and I went to his dad's house in Florida for our honeymoon. Even though we were only gone for two weeks, I got so homesick for Bry, and couldn't wait to get back home. Upon returning home, I went back to work dancing. Being a new mother and wife was not easy, but it was a step in the right direction. For the first time in my life I had something I could be a part of, a family of my very own.

Death Loses Again

I never really put into perspective how dangerous it was for me to be a dancer, especially working the late hours that I did. Little did I know at the time just how much jeopardy my life had been in all those nights dancing. I should have known that the enemy was not going to let go of me so easily, but my mindset was not on spiritual things at those moments. All I knew is that I was living my life the best way I knew how at that point.

I continued dancing to help make ends meet, and I really did make pretty good money. This one night in particular was not only a defining moment in my life, but what I'd like to call a 'divine turning point'. I was at the club, and it was a very slow night. I only had made about $100 compared to the $400 to $500 that I usually would bring home each night. I left work at about 2:00 am that night. As I drove home, I noticed a car sitting across the road with its bright lights on. I thought that it was a little peculiar for the car to just be sitting there, but I proceeded to make my way home. As soon as I drove past the car, the driver started following me. I had to drive through a couple small towns before I would reach my house, so I was nowhere near home. As I approached a four-way intersection, 'Something' (I know now that it was the Holy Spirit) told me to look at the passenger's seat and pretend like I was talking to someone. I did that in approval, but this car continued to follow me. The next light was a flashing yellow light, so I proceeded to yield, and then drove off sternly. The driver then began to flick his lights to see if there was someone else in my car. I was in complete terror as I was in the middle of nowhere with not a single other house around. As I approached my town, he continued to flash his lights. Becoming even more scared, I floored it, and he also sped up right next to me on the driver's side as though he was going to pass by me. Instead, he slowed down and got behind me again and started ramming me with his car. He continued until I ended up spinning out, facing the opposite direction on the other side of the road in a ditch.

My entire life flashed before me as he got out of his car and started walking down the ravine where my car sat. My car was locked, so when he attempted to open my door, he couldn't. So, he started kicking the window in an attempt to break the glass. I feared that if he kicked the window in, the glass would break, and I would get cut up. Oddly enough, I had been watching Oprah earlier that day and she said that if you ever find yourself in danger, you have a '30-second window' in which to think quickly and make a decision to act and get away. My decision was to pretend to be unconscious. I quickly realized that wasn't going to work. I remembered that Oprah had followed by saying, "Get out!" So, I unlocked the door to begin trying to get out.

My car was a 2-door car and the only one I could exit was the one where he was standing. The other side of the vehicle was steep into the ravine and was full of water. He tried to pull me out of the car and looked down at my seatbelt, not realizing that it was automatic. He started to get frustrated and began to hit me as he pulled me out further. I had no sharp object or weapon to defend myself. He was careful to keep his face above the car so that I could not see him. In the midst of the struggle his pants fell down, and I knew his intentions were to rape me, abduct me, kill me, or all of the above. He kept trying to hide his face so I wouldn't see it but I certainly did *not* want to see it.

I was desperate to get out of this situation alive. I grabbed a hold of his throat, squeezing as hard as I could, and he let go of me. In the distance I saw headlights approaching. To try and calm him down, I told him that I didn't see or hear anything, and that he could take my purse with all the money in it. I told him to take it and just leave me alone. In an attempt to make him leave, I warned him that the approaching vehicle would see him if he didn't get away quickly. He finally took my purse and left as I watched him go.

Survival Mode

As the other car drew closer, I ran into the woods and hid. I got all cut up and scratched because of the shorts and flip flops I had on. As I ran through the words, I stepped in mud and only God knows what else. I couldn't walk along the road in fear of him seeing me and trying to finish what he started. As I continued to walk, I approached an abandoned grain mill and bridge that I had recognized. I knew I had to cross this bridge to get home, but I was so afraid that the guy would see me crossing the bridge. But, there was no other place for me to go.

By this time, it was about 3:00am and I had seen a couple of cars pass. I stopped one of the cars. When the driver rolled down the window, I saw two gentlemen in the car. They claimed that they had just left work, but I made them turn the car light on so that I could see exactly who was in the car. I told them that I needed to get to the police station immediately.

On the way, we passed one patrol car and another police officer who was at the local liquor store making his nightly rounds. They let me out of the car so I could talk to the officer. As I proceeded to tell the officer about what had just transpired, he questioned me as though he didn't believe me. I felt like I was the perpetrator instead of the victim. He drove me to where my car was and radioed for another officer to come. They asked me if I had been drinking and questioned me about the scratches on my body. In their eyes, I was just a drunk stripper who had an accident. To make matters worse, I had given this man my purse with all my personal information in it.

How could I possibly return to 'life as usual' after all that had just transpired? I had just experienced a psychotic encounter where I was almost raped and could have been killed. My baby would have been left without a mother, and Miles would have had to raise him all alone. Add to this the fact that the predator that attacked me had all the information he needed to find me. Who knew what he really wanted or if he would strike again. For all I knew, he could be watching my house each and every night. Or worse yet, following me everywhere I went. I was absolutely paranoid and anxious beyond belief.

My step-dad Paul eventually moved in with us because he and his wife in Alabama got divorced. He had not changed a bit since the last time I had seen him. He was still a very heavy drinker and smoked marijuana every day. The same childhood I thought I had escaped from had come right to my own door this time. One night, he passed out with a cigarette in his hand and burned a hole in my new furniture. He tried to hide it, but I found it the next day. I could not allow my household to be destroyed. After all I endured throughout my young life, I refused to let my child grow up like I did. This cycle had to be broken somehow. So for the sake of my family and our safety, I had to throw him out. It was one of the hardest things I ever had to do, and it broke my heart but I asked him to leave.

I wasn't home when he moved out, but he left me a letter he had written. In the letter, he said that he was worthless and didn't have anyone that loved him. He went on to say that he considered himself a screw-up. Instead of allowing the letter to put me in a place of guilt, I realized that I had made the right decision. I had made a decision that signified that it was time for me to live for *me*, and for no one else. Miles was working again, and little by little, the anxiety associated with the attack began to cease. Once more, things seemed to be getting better, until we received a phone call that Miles' brother Eddie had been in a terrible car wreck.

Miles and I went to the hospital to meet his mom, brother, and his brother's girlfriend. We went to the family room to wait. Before we could get even remotely comfortable, Miles' family that we were supposed to meet all came out to tell us that Eddie had suffered massive trauma and had passed away. We were all in a state of shock and disbelief. Eddie had been so good to Miles and me. They allowed us to go back and see him at that time. Eddie was the one who fed me when I was sick in the hospital and now he was gone, without me even having a chance to nurture him back to life. I had never seen a dead body before and it was extremely hard. Although our relationship was not the greatest, I felt so bad for Miles's mom and really didn't have any proper words to say to her. I felt so sorry for Miles and her for losing a son, and brother. Just leave this out

Just Call Me Gomer/Trouble in Paradise

Miles and I decided to sell our trailer, and move into an apartment that was larger and had more space. By this time, Bryson was preparing to go to Kindergarten, and we didn't want to put him in public school. Miles' family were all Catholics, so his grandmother suggested a Catholic school. She even offered to pay the tuition if we elected for him to go there, so we agreed. Since I was not Catholic, I had to take catechism classes. In addition, Miles and I started to attend Catholic services while my dad took Bry to a Pentecostal Church with him. During the time Dad spent with Bry, he soon discovered that Bry knew much more about marijuana than any child should know. Needless to say, Dad was livid and threatened to take him away from Miles and me if I did not make sure that the drug activity did not occur around him.

Dad wasn't too thrilled about us going to Catholic Church either, and he certainly did not want Bry attending Catholic school. One day, he invited us to go a revival service at the Pentecostal church he attended. I was absolutely clueless to what a 'revival service' was, but Dad explained to me that it was a service where people gathered to worship the Lord. This was an experience unlike anything I had ever experienced before, so I went with him. There was such joy there throughout the whole SERVICE. At the end of the service, the pastor asked everyone to come up for prayer and have hands laid on them. Dad asked me to go down with him for prayer and I went. I thought, '"What *is* this?" It took me back to the television program I used to watch at my Grandma's house where the people ran around the church and fell out. The next thing I knew, people starting 'laying out' on the floor. When it was my Dad's turn to receive prayer, the pastor did not even touch him, and he went out. Then it was my turn, and when the pastor's hands touched me, I was out! I felt such indescribable warmth. Although I wanted to get up, I couldn't move. I couldn't even open my eyes. When I was finally able to get up, I was on fire. I could not wait to get home to tell Miles. This was better than any drug I ever had, and I wanted more.

Back at home, I had the best husband a woman could ask for. Miles was a very loving and romantic man. He cooked for me, prepared candle light dinners, ran my bath water, and put rose petals on the floor leading up to the bedroom. He was a God-sent to make me a better person; but yet, I was on a path of self-destruction. I honestly felt like I didn't deserve him. In addition, there was the added pressure of our contradicting work shifts. We didn't see each other a whole lot, but he was good to me every moment that we did. What did I do to deserve such a good man? Miles and I had been married for four years, and our happiness was just too good to be true. I had never been so happy before, until I met Miles. My pattern was always to expect bad things to happen when things were going well, because good things never happened to me. So my question became, "When was the floor going to fall from beneath me? My vision was, I might as well screw this up because it wasn't going to last anyway. Getting married did not deal with the root issues that were deep inside my heart. On my first act of self-destruction I cheated on Miles with his band-mate, Sam. Right after the incident, I went home and told him what I had done. I was so sick, both mentally and physically. I begged him for forgiveness, and he was very loving and forgiving. I hated myself and felt so ashamed. Miles, being the kind-hearted man I knew he was, thanked me for being honest with him and asked me if there was anything he was doing wrong. He questioned if he was good enough for me and I honestly did not know how to answer him. He assured me that we would get through it. He proved once again that I did not deserve him. I honestly thought that my infidelity would be the end of our marriage, but God had other plans. I vowed to do everything I could to show Miles that I loved and appreciated him. I was determined to do everything in my power to make our marriage work. I stayed home and took care of our son and our home so that Miles didn't have to worry or stress.

Shortly after, we learned that the owner of the apartment house we lived in had put it up for sale. We had 30 days to find a new place to live. At this point, I was ready to move, so we began looking right away. Dad was still very adamant about Bryson not going to Catholic school and I could not let go of the Power of God that touched my life in that Revival. We found a house out in the middle of the country and I listen to Dad and sent Bry to start Kindergarten in a new school. In addition, I found a job to help Miles so that he would not have so much pressure and financial strain.

Little by little, the trust began to be rebuilt between us. We worked opposite shifts again, so in order to communicate with each other, we wrote notes and left them for one another to see. Although we were trying our best to work on our marriage the best way we knew how, we were barely holding on. In addition to the lack of communication, we began to have issues with intimacy. Whenever we came together, I would experience excruciating pain. There was no pleasure in it at *all*. I was honestly convinced that this was something that I brought on myself, like something that I was being punished for because of my infidelity. It was already bad enough that we hardly saw each other, but whenever we did, I had no interest in being intimate because of the pain. We began to disconnect because he had needs that I could not fulfill. I was afraid to go to the doctor and kept putting off making an appointment to get checked out. To add on to the problems, I did not feel like Miles was being compassionate or understanding toward me. Ultimately, the lack of intimacy devastated our marriage.

At work, I met a guy who was out on work release. He and I began to hang out after work. However because of the stipulations of his work release program, we didn't spend a lot of time together. He had to return to jail immediately after his shift was over. We did talk to each other on the phone whenever we got the chance. Meanwhile, my step-brother William and I started to hang out again. As you may remember William was Greg's son. Whenever I'd go to visit my mom, I would see him. In addition, he started to come over to my house after work. I felt alone and needed someone to talk to so I opened up to him about the marital problems I was having. In the midst of our heartfelt talks he confessed that he liked me when we were younger. We ended up having sexual relations, *without pain*. So, I thought that whatever the problem was with me and Miles had now ended. I didn't even bother to tell him because he was being uncompassionate, so I was going to be selfish too. William and I continued to see each other, and in return Miles and I argued constantly. He wanted to talk, but I didn't want to. I would actually always escalate the arguments and become physical with him. I told him that we weren't working, and that he had to move out. Deep down I didn't want him to move but eventually, he did move.

My cousin moved in with me, and I continued to see William. After a while, it became too expensive for us to live there, so I took Bry out of school. My cousin moved in with a friend of hers, and I moved in with William at his grandmother's house. Miles and I worked out a visitation agreement where he would get Bry every other weekend. Miles moved back into the house and finished out the lease so Bry actually never fully moved out of the house at that time.

The happy little family that I had been blessed with such a short time before was now divided I didn't, and couldn't feel the magnitude of what had happened. All I knew was that I had to survive emotionally. Although William and I lived together, there was no love between us. It really was a matter of convenience for me. Physically, he provided a roof for me and Bry to live under. Emotionally, he filled a void, or at least I tried to fill the void with him. Whenever we were intimate, the pain started to resurface. Knowing it wasn't just Miles, I finally gave in and went to the doctor. After examining me, the doctor wanted to perform a microscopic exploratory procedure. The very thought of surgery freaked me out, so I called Miles and let him know what was going on. He agreed to be there for me because I was scared. After all that Miles and I had been through, we still loved each other.

It was a same-day procedure that required that I stay for a few hours afterwards to be monitored. The doctors discovered scar tissue and hard cysts on my uterus and also removed my appendix. I had to be on bed rest for a couple days afterward in the hospital. When I was discharged, Miles took me to his house and took care of me for a couple days as I recovered. In the meantime, William was furious because I was leaning on Miles for comfort and companionship. What he didn't understand was that Miles was filing for divorce and was just helping me through the recovery process.

We divorced peacefully because we just wanted to dissolve the marriage. We came together and compromised with what we both wanted and just like that it was over. My dad cried and blamed me for the divorce. He said that it was my fault and I had caused it. I think more than anything, he was very hurt and disappointed in me. He pleaded with me to work things out with Miles. However at this point, my mind was made up. He didn't know what went on in my house so the way I looked at it, he couldn't judge me.

Exhausted With Life –

Dissociative Identity Disorder

William and I moved into our own place, and things seemed to be going pretty well for a while. Just then William started hanging out late after work and would never come straight home. He was spending a lot of money drinking, and was very irresponsible. I was 27 and he had no respect for the fact that I had a child to raise. Although I didn't see any sign of what he was doing, I later learned that he was doing hardcore drugs.

Now, in the beginning of this book, I told you that we would revisit dissociative identity disorder, and this is the perfect time to do just that. Dissociative identity disorder, also known as multiple personality disorder or split personality disorder, is defined as a mental disorder that is characterized by two or more personalities that control a person's behavior and is accompanied by memory loss. Under stress or duress, the individual's personality literally 'splits', revealing character traits of other people who manifest in order to defend or protect the person.

There were constantly physical confrontations between William and I, during which I would dissociate into an enraged male personality named Henry. Things got so violent when I split that I actually once knocked one of William's front teeth loose. Things got so bad with William and me that I actually did not want to go home to him. We were fighting before work and I had no intentions to continue fighting after work, so I decided not to go home. Instead, I went to a bar with my mom and cousin and got drunk. I knew that if I went home, we'd fight again, and I would be defenseless; so I called my supervisor and told him what happened. He allowed me to sleep on his couch that night.

My mom took me to my supervisor's house and picked me up the next morning. On the way home, she informed me that William went into a blind rage and had flattened my car tires. She continued to explain that he tore up the house and shot up my mailbox. She insisted that I needed to get home as soon as possible to try to handle the issue. Apparently, William had lost it because I stayed out that night. I was anxious and afraid, and I had no clue of what I was getting ready to walk in on when I pulled into the driveway. When Mom and I arrived at the house, I saw the shots in the mailbox and the flat tires that she had warned me about. My mattress was outside drying because he had urinated all over it, and Mom had washed it. He came over and was very irate, but I spoke to him very calmly. I tried to explain to him that I didn't want to come home intoxicated while he and I were not getting along. I continued to let him know that I wanted to break up, but I knew I could not afford to maintain the house by myself financially. I found a new job that paid more, and things just went from bad to worse between the two of us. He drank and drugged harder, and we eventually broke up. I decided to just do my own thing.

I went partying at a bar one night and ended up going home Sam. Yes, the same Sam I had cheated with before. We had a one-night stand that night and used protection. However, around this same time, I had unprotected sex with William. A month later, I missed my period. When I took a pregnancy test, it was positive and I was pregnant. I informed both William and Sam at that time about the results. William insisted that the baby was his, and I let him know that I wasn't too sure exactly who the father was. He said that he was going to move back in with me and help me whether the baby was his or not, and I let him move back in. But Miles and I always talked to each other, and I let him know what I was going through with William and Sam also. Although William would not change, I needed him there. The doctors immediately decided that because of complications I had during childbirth before, I needed to have a C-section with this birth also. I was so tired and exhausted with life. I couldn't take anymore and wanted to give up.

Restoration Begins-Mariska

I was so worn out, beat up, tired, exhausted, and broken. That's exactly where God needed me to be so that I could surrender. I started going to the Pentecostal Church with Dad again. I tried to get William to go with me, but he refused, so I kept going by myself and *for* myself. I got baptized in 1999. The Lord kept pulling at me as the Holy Spirit began to woo me into this beautiful new world called Salvation. At home, I would just lay across my bed and cry out to Jesus. Spending time alone with God was very special to me. He would manifest His Presence and give me such peace. He would embrace me and wipe my tears away. I didn't want to have another baby without Him in my life and I needed Him now more than ever. I was tired of straddling and teeter-tottering back and forth between giving my life to Him or not. The Lord told me that if I kept my eyes on Him, He would restore everything the enemy had stolen from me.

As scheduled, I was admitted into the hospital on January 13, 2000 for the C-section, and William was with me during the surgery. My baby came out yelling and screaming, happy and healthy! I was ecstatic. I had a precious baby girl, Mariska, on that very special day. I was especially happy because I would be able to bond with her better than I could with Bry. William was going to sign the birth certificate, but his mother advised him to wait until he was sure that he was the father. When he left the hospital, to my surprise, Miles came to see me also. I welcomed his visits and began to see how wonderful of a person he really was and just how much he genuinely loved me this entire time.

Upon my release from the hospital, I was happy to bring Mariska home to the family. In the midst of all the joy of bringing her home, the question of paternity still needed to be dealt with. When the results of the paternity test came in the mail, William and I were still living together. The test revealed that he was not Mariska's father. He was very disappointed and angry, and he immediately moved out. I contacted Sam and let him know that he needed to come and be tested. He agreed and met Mariska, now four months old, and I at the hospital where they conducted a mouth swab. The test confirmed that he was the father. He was very cooperative as we went to court to establish paternity and begin child support.

I found a job and worked during the day while Mom watched Mariska, and Bry attended school. I continued to attend church each and every Sunday. Miles and I still kept in touch, and he began to comment on the big change he saw in me and my lifestyle. I was so happy to tell him that I had been going to church. To my delight, he asked if he could come with me. I reminded him that it was a Pentecostal Church but he didn't care, he still wanted to go. We began to attend services together more frequently on the weekends when he had Bry. The Lord began to do a great work in Miles, just like he had done in me. The changes God was making in him were evident. Soon, he served on the praise and worship team, and I sang on the choir. God was working in the both of us and made us so involved with our presence in the church. We abstained from being intimate and focused on the Lord.

One day, when the call for salvation was made, Bry went up to the front of the church to receive salvation. The church offered baptism, and I wanted to rededicate myself. So, I signed up for Bry and me to be baptized. I convinced Miles that Bry was old enough and he decided that he wanted to be baptized right along with us. The Lord was performing a work of reconciliation and restoration right in front of our eyes. It was clear and evident that Miles and I still had feelings of genuine love for one another. He was determined that he was going to seek the Lord concerning his feelings and see what His will for us would be.

In another effort to make improvements on our life, we began to seek counseling from out pastor. During the sessions, we began to revisit issues in our past, and he ministered to us on how to build our marriage on God's Foundation. We laid all our baggage before the Lord including: my childhood, my relationship with my mother, infidelity, and so much more. Miles and I were committed to learning how to walk in covenant with the Lord. When the pastor asked us when we wanted to get married, we chose July 13, 2001. On that day we were set to be *re*married, only this time was going to be 'until death do us part.'

I Do Again/Tests and Trials

Miles took me ring shopping, and I was on cloud nine. It was so refreshing to have the Lord in the midst of us ordering our new steps. We were not sexually active, and we did not live together. We were both determined to do it *God's* Way this time around. When he proposed, he took me out to a place along the river, sat me on a log, and asked me to marry him. Of course, I told him yes. Our marriage was restored and we got married on that very day of July 13th. Our entire family was elated, especially Dad! Mariska was our flower girl, and Dad walked me down the aisle again. Mom and my step-dad Greg would not come, but they were happy for us nonetheless.

Our honeymoon started at a bed and breakfast, before setting off for Michigan for a few days. When we returned home, Miles moved back in with me. We lived together in that house, going strong, for about a year until we moved into the house we still reside in today. Meanwhile in church, we were growing and being blessed. We were learning more and more about the Lord and seeing and experiencing Him in a personal way. However, we began to become stagnant and stunted in our spiritual growth. Don't get me wrong, I was, and still am, eternally grateful to the Lord for how He used my Dad to introduce me to the Holy Spirit. But, he served on the board of the church, and things began to become a little too political. We stopped attending the church for a while as we sought the Lord for a new direction.

At this point, I could honestly say that I had a real relationship with God. I was growing in the knowledge of who He is and learning, day by day, to trust Him more. As I grew in the Word, I began to be stretched in ways that I did not think I would be able to endure. Trials began to come my way, and I had to learn to walk by faith. The first trial was when we learned that my mom had been battling hepatitis C. The doctors offered her experimental treatment, but she was very skeptical about trying it. Her liver was severely damaged and continued to deteriorate. Bottom line was, she needed a transplant. While she was placed on the transplant list, the doctors gave her medications that were designed to stop the progression of any further liver damage. It was so difficult for me to watch my mom, who was once so strong, turn into this weak, frail woman. During this time my paternal grandmother was not doing well either. To make matters worse, Paul had developed melanoma cancer. I felt like my world was caving in after being built so strong. To try and escape the pain of what was going on, I spent a lot of time on the internet playing games. During this time, I developed friendships by chatting with people online. This helped me to cope with the stress of what was going on in real life. I felt a great deal of pressure from Miles to be intimate, but my mind just wasn't there. Once again, I felt disconnected from him.

Online, I met a young man from Detroit named Chad, who had just broken up with his fiancée. I shared what I was going through with Chad. Again, I was in a lonely place, longing for comfort. Miles never dealt with stressful situations well and communicating with him was difficult. He would just shut down completely. I told him that if he needed to 'go elsewhere' for sexual relations, I would understand, as long as he didn't let me or our children find out. This was one of the worse points I had ever experienced in my entire life, and intimacy was the last thing on my mind.

My online friend Chad and I became friends, and I went to Detroit to spend a few days with him. Believe it or not, our relationship was purely platonic. I just needed to get away from all the negative aspects in my life. Grandma, Mom, and my step-dad were dying, and there was nothing I could do about it. These were three of the strongest people I knew, and they were on the verge of leaving me. My friendship with Chad gave me a place to escape to. We communicated through Yahoo messenger and by phone when I was at home. I would write to him and occasionally, I visited him every once in a while. Miles knew about my friendship with Chad, but he turned a blind eye to it. One day, I decided to take Mariska with me to visit him and we stayed for an entire week. During our visit, she saw us kiss. Once we returned home, I went back to visit him for a weekend alone. While I was away, my sister and cousin knew that things weren't going well with Miles and me. They came and visited Miles to get him high. Also while I was gone, Mariska told him that she "saw Mommy kiss her friend."

Everything seemed ok, like nothing was even said, when I got back home. Two weeks later, I left Mariska with Mom and returned to Detroit. I again stayed for a week, and Chad and I were intimate. I had no intimate feelings for him at all; but I was hurting, and he was there. Running away had always worked for me before, so I pondered leaving Indiana. Chad advised me not to do it because he told me that we were both trying to cover up what we were going through emotionally. He also informed me that he was going to reconcile with his fiancée, and that I should go back to Indiana.

My friend bought me a bus ticket, and Mom and our cousin picked me up from the station. Mom began to question me about my behavior, and I let her know that I could not deal with the pressure of her being sick. I arrived home to find out that Miles slept with my cousin, in our house. His reasoning and justification was that I told him that he could do whatever he wanted, so he did.

The truth be told, I *did* say that, but my cousin? He was hurting and he wanted to hurt me in the same way. We agreed to try to do our best to work things out, and God kept us together. We needed to give our marriage another shot. We didn't want to hurt our children, and we didn't want to hurt God anymore.

Family Feud

There is some truth to the saying 'when it rains, it pours.' It seemed as though the rain just would not stop in my life. Grandma had a heart attack. When I went to visit her, the doctors said that she had been through a lot and that she needed to rest. Her condition was 'touch and go'. Our family left and came back later that evening to check on her; we needed to stay close by her. When I went home, I could not rest. So, I went back to the hospital to sit in the waiting room. Even though I wasn't able to see her, I just had to be there.

When I arrived back at the hospital, the family was in an uproar, fussing and fighting. I, along with Mariska, went into the waiting room. Dad and his wife were also there. He asked me what I was doing there. Then, right in front of Mariska, my step-mom began to berate me about how bad of a mother I was, among other things. I told her that this was not the time or the place for what she was trying to do, or the points she was trying to make. I decided to take Mariska home and return back to the hospital by myself. I spent almost every night there for about a week until Grandma passed away. Before she closed her eyes, she told us that she saw Jesus pull up in a white car. She also shared with us that she told Him that He had to wait because she had to tell her son goodbye. She described the flowers she saw and a party they were preparing for her. She waited until her son arrived from Florida. She was moved to another room, and the next day, she went Home to be with her savior.

After Grandma's death, two months had passed and Mom grew much worse. Her body began to fill up with ammonia, her liver became toxic, and she began to hallucinate. She stayed in the intensive care unit while her name was on the transplant list in Chicago. The doctors in Indiana reported to the doctors in Chicago, giving updates on Mom's condition. The levels of toxins in her body eventually lowered, and she was released to go home. However, she began to lose her mind and fell into a depression. I tried so hard to fight through this, and I continued to work. Then, one night, she called me and said that she had to get to Chicago right away because a liver had been found. She had been on the waiting list for quite a while, so the whole family was filled with hope and anticipation.

She decided to take the trip to Chicago with my Dad. My sister and I made plans to meet them in there as soon as we could. We arrived a few hours after her successful transplant surgery. After the surgery, fluid began to build up in her lungs; so she underwent another procedure to drain the fluid. I was responsible for consenting on behalf of Mom so that she could have the surgery. My step-dad was exhausted, so I told him to leave and come back later. My sister and I stayed to relieve him, and give Mom support.

Meanwhile, my sister told me that she was going to leave and come back later she had arranged for a guy friend of hers to come and pick her up. I stayed with Mom, and watched her pulled through the procedure well. Hours passed, and my sister had not come back yet. I began to worry about her because I had no idea where she was or what company she was keeping. Anything could have happened to her, as I rightfully have discovered in life. She did not return for about ten hours so I called my step-dad. As soon as I hung up, she walked into the room. She was high, and I was furious. I couldn't contain myself and we began to argue. She then had the audacity to ask the nurse to put our family in a hotel because she needed a bed. I told her to get out of the room because I was disgusted with her. Mom started to wake up, and I was crying profusely. I tried to calm down and be strong for Mom. The last thing I needed was for Mom to regress after she had made so much progress. I spent a few more nights with her there at the hospital. Eventually, my sister and I booked a hotel room for a night, and then we set to return home.

During the drive home, I could not talk to her. I didn't even want to be around her. Paul called me to check on Mom, and I gladly updated him on her progress. I told him that I really loved him and that I really wanted to see him, but I couldn't bear to see him sick and suffering. I let him know that it was especially difficult with all that Mom was enduring and because of Grandma being gone. He understood and agreed that he didn't feel it was a good idea for me to see him the way he was. He had lost all his hair and a tremendous amount of weight. To add to the chaos, my sister and my brother were overtaken by their meth addiction. My brother did, however, at least try and take care of his dad. Mom stayed in Chicago for a month so that she could continue to receive services and therapy as an outpatient. Then finally, she was able to return home.

By His Stripes

I was at a very difficult place in my life, what I thought as a fork in the road. I had a decision to make. Either I was going to give up and allow Satan to trick me into giving up, or I was going to trust that the same Jesus Who visited me in the hospital and raised me from the dead was going to walk me through this valley. I was severely depressed and deeply saddened that so much was taking place all at once. Thankfully, Mom was well on her way to recovery now. In contrast though, Paul was losing his battle against melanoma and had passed away. In the midst of all this, Miles had been with my cousin and also someone else sexually. Even though I told him it was ok, and I had been intimate with Chad, I didn't know how to deal with this added stress. It was too overwhelming and I began to stop eating and I lost a lot of weight. Miles suggested counseling, but because of my past experience with the prescription meds that came with the counseling, I refused to go. However things kept going downhill, so I eventually agreed to seek counseling with Miles.

God blessed us with a Christian counselor named Dr. Jay. As he counseled us, we went through an extensive process where we were challenged to get to the root of what was happening between us and the reasons why. During this time, I was officially diagnosed with Dissociative Identity Disorder. There were a total of five personalities that would come out whenever I felt the pressure or strain of trying to deal with certain things going on in my life. One personality was 'born' when I was molested at such a young age. The other came about when I got raped the first time. One spilt from those two, and another was born. The fourth personality came when Peter beat me and threatened my life. The final one was born when I was raped by Kirk. I had no idea that I even had different personalities, but I thought I was fine. I didn't even know when one would become active. As I began to go deeper in counseling, Dr. Jay implemented hypnosis. The hypnosis enabled him to see the personalities emerge, and gave him more insight into helping me learn how to be aware of their presence and stop them from taking control when bad things would happen. I learned how to recognize triggers that would make the personalities come out, and I also learned how to better handle situations in my everyday life. Dr. Jay was truly sent to me straight from God. He really helped Miles and I make sense of everything that we had endured. My disorder wasn't an excuse for my behavior, neither was it a means for me to justify the choices I made, but it was such a relief to get to the underlying cause of all the problems I was having. All these years, I knew there was something wrong with me because I would literally lose chunks of time in my life. People would come back and tell me things that I had done or said and I would not remember a single moment of it. I would also misplace things very often. Throughout my entire life, I felt like I was losing my mind. Doing drugs just made matters worse, but now I had the tools necessary to heal; build my marriage and family; and honor the Lord with my life. Miles and I saw Dr. Jay for quite some time. Our sessions were occurring less often as we got further along and more accomplished. Initially, we went twice a week. Then, we went once a week. Eventually, it was just me and I was able to go just twice a month, and finally down to just once a month. For the first time in a *long* time I was making consistent progress, and it felt great!

I was grateful that God had stepped in and helped me regain mental and emotional stability. Miles and I had not been in a church for quite a while. My Dad's son was going to pastoral school and preparing to pastor a church that was offered to him. When he started his church, we went and attended right along with him. I was happy to be back in church again. Miles fell right in place on the praise and worship team, and again, I found my place in the choir. My step-brother asked Miles to start the youth ministry. In addition, Mom and Greg began attending. Mom and Greg, along with sister Tiffany, were even baptized. Also, Tiffany's baby was dedicated to the Lord. Greg even joined the praise and worship team. The Lord was truly blessing both of my families. One Sunday, we were driving to church when Miles asked me when I would be going back to see Dr. Jay. I told him that I had been healed by Jesus. I did not even realize that I said it until afterwards. I don't even know exactly *when* He healed me of this disorder, but I *knew* I was healed.

Now, I'm sure that you've heard someone say before that there is no perfect church, and that is true. In the midst of all the Lord was doing to bring healing and restoration to my family, the enemy began to raise his head at us. One day, my brother preached a message dealing with horoscopes and astrology. This caused my step-dad to become very upset and left the church. Mom continued to visit every now and then but it was not the same as it was such a short time before. Problems continued at the church as the Lord began to call Miles and I to outreach ministry. We were on fire and willing to step out and do what the Lord was placing on our hands and in our hearts. He began to speak to us about starting a food pantry, and also began to deal with us about witnessing and listening to souls door to door. The name of the ministry God was giving us was called "Jesus is Knocking Ministry". My brother rejected the idea and made me become very unhappy at the church. This was upsetting because, although I had seen some unsettling things that he was doing, my family and I continued to serve and support him. After much prayer and seeking the Lord, Miles and I had a meeting with him and informed him that we were leaving his church. My brother tried to convince us to come back, but the Lord didn't lead us that way and revealed several things that confirmed that it was time for us to move on. When I asked him why he would not allow us to do outreach, he said that he was afraid that too many people would come to the church and he wouldn't know what to do with them. I thought that this didn't make much since because it would allow him to preach to all those people and make an impact in all of their lives, but my brother had other thoughts.

Shortly after this, God moved us to another church, and it was awesome! The pastor and congregants at the new church were so loving and caring towards me. I was totally free to worship, dance, shout, and enjoy the Lord in any way I knew how. So many new experiences with the Lord began to come forth at this new church. At our time of arrival, the pastor was looking for another pastor to come replace him. He found a younger pastor, and he and his wife came to lead the church. The new pastor played guitar and immediately connected with Miles. Bry loved church and enjoyed worship. It made me so happy to see him expressing his love for God at such a young age. I was especially intrigued because the pastor had a heart for door to door ministry and planned to start street ministry like Miles and I had previously talked about. I was so happy to see everything the Lord had spoken to me in the previous church beginning to unfold at this new one. The Lord did a quick work in us and we were flourishing. It was my pleasure to pray for people and serve the community in every means I could.

One day, the pastor's overseer came and held a service for us. At the end of the service, he spoke a prophetic Word over me. This Word read as follows:

"Ye have not chosen me, but I have chosen you and ordained you, that ye should go and bring forth fruit, and that your fruit should remain: that whatsoever ye shall ask of the Father in My Name, He may give it you. I am meeting you in this appointment now, for this is the appointed time and ordained time for you to receive from me as never before. For it's been spoken, saith the Lord, that you have received my anointing and yes, you have asked, but notice that I am calling you to a level of understanding that you have never experienced before. It does not have anything to do with what you have done, but it has to do with what I am about to do in your life and the lives that I send to you, those you have relationships with now, and those that are coming. For now, saith the Lord, I am going to cause you to publish My Word. I am going to cause My Doctrine to fall upon you as the gentle rain. I am going to call you and lead you about by My Spirit in such a way that you will know, under every circumstance, when I am speaking to you and blessing you. I will cause you to walk upon the high places and eat of the honey and drink of the milk, for it is time and timely, saith the Lord that you come to me in that intimacy of our new relationship, for I am causing you to be a repairer of the breach. I'm causing you to come into deeper fellowship with Me. I am interrupting the breach that the world has placed in your life and brining you wholly into Me now in a Kingdom setting. Know this, saith the Lord, that this is just the beginning of what you have actually asked Me for. For you have asked me, now I am responding before this witness of people. You will begin to see me move in ways that you never expected to see me move. For even the prayers of hope that you have prayed in the past now become prayers of faith that bear fruit. No matter what you ask in My Name, you will see it performed, for My Anointing is upon you. My Love is for you. My Good is for you, and this is just *the beginning, for not only will you repair the breach, but you must be the message. So, now I am bringing you to a place of restoration, a place of restoration that you have asked for, a place of restoration that brings fullness and completeness, a place of rest that brings peace and not sorrow, and beauty for ashes. I am causing My praise to well up in you in such a way that you will be a witness. I will use you to be a witness to the uttermost on My behalf, saith the Lord. For the anointing you carry and the anointing you seek will give you the ability to know who to pray for, who to heal, who to deliver, and who to set free. For, indeed I am ushering My ambassadorship to you now, that you might fully understand more of what it is that I am doing."*

The Lord instructed me to get a copy of the service and write down what He spoke over me word for word. Shortly after, the Lord instructed me to go to Dennis Cramer's class and also pay for my spiritual grandmother to attend with me. Dennis Cramer is a prophet and seer who hosts schools of prophecy all over the nation. We went to a class he was conducting, and it was one of the greatest experiences I have ever had in my life. I learned so much about prophecy. Under the leading of the Holy Ghost, I went with my spiritual grandmother to various women's meetings and traveled with her extensively.

Back at the church, things began to shift. The Spirit of the Lord revealed that there was a spirit of division trying to split the church. The Lord wanted to rid the church of the debt that was owed on the building. The pastor insisted that we, the people, were the Church and that we didn't need a 'building' at all. So, we began to have service in one couple's home. This caused a great deal of division because many of the people didn't want to let go of the building they had helped to build. The former pastor, along with many of the long-time members, left the church and things were going haywire. Miles and I really needed to believe in what the Lord was saying. We loved both pastors, and we had to separate from our emotions to them. The Lord did not release us to join another church. He assured us that we were the Church and that we were to come together in the Word and seek Him for direction.

Round and Round on the Potter's Wheel

Miles and I visited churches here and there, but the anointing was missing. We continued to seek the Lord and studied the Word at home. At the same time, I began to experience strange changes in my body that caused me great concern. I noticed that I was unusually fatigued and could not stay up more than a couple hours at a time. So, I made an appointment to have a physical exam. The doctor diagnosed me with a thyroid disorder and placed me on medications that would take about a year to regulate my thyroid levels. In addition, my iron was very low. I was prescribed iron supplements, but they were not working. I was sent to a hematologist for further follow-up but she too could not find anything wrong. The hematologist did decide to give me iron infusions intravenously. I received ten infusions, but after the follow-up, my iron levels were completely depleted. She began to focus on my menstrual cycle referred me to a gynecologist. My menstruations had been very heavy and concerned the gynecologist. So, the gynecologist performed an ultrasound and gave me three options: take birth control, have a dilation and curettage, (D&C -a diagnostic procedure and treatment conducted in a woman's uterus), or have a partial hysterectomy. I knew I had to do something, so I opted to have the D&C done as an outpatient. I was released to go home the same day and I have not had a menstrual period, or any problems with my iron since that very day.

I had gained thirty pounds because of my thyroid imbalance, and I still wasn't feeling one hundred percent in my body. I decided to diet and exercise and I lost nine pounds fairly quickly. I felt wonderful, but I eventually hit a brick wall where I couldn't lose anymore pounds. Although I tried other diets and forms of exercise, nothing worked. One day Miles' uncle, who was very heavily involved with politics and wanted to rally support for the upcoming election, hosted a democratic party. I borrowed a dress from my friend Chloe so that I could attend. It fit, but it was very snug. She shared with me that she had started this 'wrap business' where she sold body wraps that claimed to tighten, tone, and firm the abdomen within 45 minutes. Having tried everything else, I asked her if I could buy one from her. I had a dinner to attend in a couple of weeks, so I was very much interested in trying the wraps. To my delight, she wrapped me on the spot with one of her wraps. After forty-five minutes, I was bloated and I couldn't understand why. I later learned that it was because everyone's body is different and there were different results for everyone. Chloe explained to me that I needed to wait for three days and check again. After the three days I checked and had seen amazing results. She gave me a sample of another product she sold called Greens, and it too was awesome. I felt rejuvenated and had more energy from the first dose I took. I was so intrigued that I called her and asked her to tell me what I needed to do to get more of the product. I could not afford to purchase the products for me or my household, so she suggested that I become a distributor of the product. This would allow me to not only enjoy the benefits of using the product, but also earn extra income at the same time. I told her that I would pray about it, and Miles and I each lifted the matter before the Lord during our individual prayer time. The Lord spoke to both of us, and instructed us to sign up and 'jump all in'. By faith, I used the money that I had set aside for the electric bill to sign up. I sold my first box of wraps before I even received my starter kit. Afterward, I needed to purchase three more boxes, so I used my mortgage money to purchase a booster pack. Within five weeks, I sold nine boxes, paid my electric and mortgage bills, and had some profits. I acquired seven loyal customers and two distributors of my own within those five weeks. I knew that this was a 'God-thing', and we were being blessed by him.

Starting this business was a blessing that I did not foresee. Not only was I on my way to better health, but I was able to be a blessing in helping to point others in the right direction concerning their own health and well-being. Miles always had a passion for physical fitness so he was very supportive and helpful to me in this. In the midst of our moving forward, we were hit with blows that challenged our faith. Miles' step-mother, Mandy, developed breast cancer but was treated with successful results. Her cancer was gone, however, shortly after she developed pancreatic cancer. She eventually passed away on Super bowl Sunday 2012. Two weeks later, Miles' paternal aunt committed suicide by locking herself in a camper and setting it on fire. Our family was being shaken in front of our eyes.

To make matters worse, on Easter Sunday my Dad had friends of ours over for church fellowship and family dinner. Mariska was with them and came home very hurt and upset. Apparently I was the topic of discussion, so I confronted my step-brother and step-sister. Out of anger, I let them know that they were not my real siblings and that their real father was dead. I had found this out a couple of months prior; and I had absolutely no intention of disclosing this, but my anger got the best of me at that moment. I was hurt by the fact that my Dad was not in my life for the first 19 years, but he was very active with them. I was hurt by what they did at that dinner, and I wanted them to feel the same way. What I did was horrible, and I knew that I had broken the Lord's heart by my behavior. This led me to feel very heartbroken weeks afterward. The Lord let me know that although the truth needed to be told, the way that it was done was not the right way of doing it. Mariska had also told me that they had said many negative things at dinner about seeing all of my posts about my business on Facebook. So, I quickly removed them from my Facebook page. Dad said that we were all his children and that he loved us all, but that did very little to ease my pain at this troubled time.

Shortly after, I learned that my aunt Kerry had only a short time to live. She had liver cancer and she did pass away six months later. To continue the rough patch, Miles' great-aunt passed away a virtually the same time. My new business that I loved so much began to crumble, but the Lord told me to stand strong, be still, and wait. This was a test of my faith that was only going to make me stronger and teach me to depend solely upon Him.

The Lord laid it on my heart to begin to study about the biblical principles of first fruits, the Law of Prosperity, and partnership. He began to minister us about House of Hope and the importance of sowing into the lives of Holocaust survivors. Miles and I were as blessed as the Lord filled us up with His Word and Kingdom principles. The Holy Spirit instructed me to shut down my Facebook page for two months so that I could spend time in His presence. He led Miles and me to Creflo Dollar and Kenneth Copeland's ministries. In obedience, we began to sow seed. Through these ministries, we learned how to walk by faith and stand on the Word of God no matter what stood in the way.

As should be expected, whenever the Lord began to move and bless us, the enemy was close by. The enemy was lurking and waiting for an opening to come in. As I look back on this time in my life, I can see how the Lord, in His Providence and Infinite Wisdom, allowed test after test after test to teach me how to trust

Him. He taught me how to stand in faith, and to allow Him to do a deep work within me, as well as in my family. The enemy appeared when Miles and I were invited to a party and someone there had marijuana. We smoked and ended up purchasing some for ourselves. Things began to spiral completely out of control. We found ourselves in and out of battles with marijuana use, and it became a big problem in our lives. Why were we allowing the enemy to pull us from where the Lord had restored us? Personally, I was completely derailed, so Miles and I agreed that we were done with it. Step by step, we knew that we were being preserved by the Hand of the Lord. I did not want this part of my life to resurface, and I could not understand why we couldn't resist the temptation. The Lord was so faithful in ministering to us and letting us know that He does not condemn us. I wondered if Miles felt any condemnation like I did, because I felt it so heavily. As I spent more time in the Word, I gained strength and courage to stand against condemnation. The Holy Spirit reminded me of the Word that was spoken over me in 2007 and instructed me to confess it over my life daily.

True Prosperity

As I confessed the Word of God over my life and continued to seek Him, he began a marvelous work of restoration. In January of 2013, the Lord birthed an online ministry through me; re-strategized my business with marketing and advertising tools; and taught me how to restructure my budget. One weekend, I placed an ad on a three dollar per day budget, and over 3000 people were added to my ministry page. I felt like I had just hit the lottery! God did it for me and in return I promised to pray over the people and post His Word whenever and however He told me to. I made myself available for the Lord to go to work through me.

One day, Miles' co-worker invited us to a wonderful church fellowship called the Great Banquet. It was a 72 hour shut-in with the Lord, where Believers gather to worship; pray; and share their testimonies. We were as grateful for Miles' co-worker as he was a Man of God and sponsored us at the Great Banquet. There were separate meetings for the men, so Miles went first and I interceded for him. The Lord told me that I was going to have a new husband; and when he came home, I could clearly see that the Lord had done something miraculous in him. The Glory of God was on him, and it was evident. I wanted to know all about his experience, but he wanted me to be surprised so he wouldn't tell me too much. I couldn't wait to go!

It was time for the women to meet, and when I went, the Lord kept confirming His Word to me. This was such an extraordinary experience as I began to see God move in ways I never thought possible. I began to see the Lord's Face in place of all the people that were present with me. I wanted to burst and share, but the Lord told me to fan the Glory over them, and I did as He instructed. This was one encounter with the Lord that I would never forget for the rest of my life.

We took a break for snack and had prayer with leaders and counselors who were there. I asked them if I could pray with them in private, and they obliged. The Lord led me to share the testimony about the business and ministry He birthed in my life. By this point, I had about 8,000 people on the ministry page, and I gave God all the Glory for what He had done. The next day, during the closing ceremony, the room was packed full of people. Everyone came in and stood on the platform, and the manifestation of God's presence and Glory was phenomenal. The men sang to us. I was on fire and boasted about how Miles and I were flourishing in our marriage. While we were there, Miles and I set up a schedule where we would spend one evening together speaking Word confessions and watching ministry teachings.

Breaking the Bloodline Curse

When Bryson turned 21, I almost had to pinch myself. I couldn't believe how quickly he had become a man. With the adult title, he was ready to prove how much of a man he *thought* he was. He was in college and informed me that he was going to have fun and pretty much 'do his own thing'. I let him know that it would only last for a certain amount of time. As frustrated as I was with him, the Lord told me to take my hands off of him and trust Him to take care of Bry, just like he took care of me.

It wasn't easy watching Bry go down a similar path that I had previously traveled, because I knew all too well the pain, the hurt, and the struggle of what I had endured. But I held fast to what the Lord said. He started to party, drink, and experiment with drugs, and in turn became very distant and began ignoring my phone calls. One day, he called me and told me that he had heard a very loud sound on his way to work, but he didn't know what it was. He later realized, after he left work, that there was a bullet hole in the back of his car. He was panicked, but I had peace and calmly asked him about the condition of the car. He became very frustrated because I was not worrying and fussing over him, and he demanded to speak to his dad.

During this time, Bry met a girl named Avery and had sexual relations with her. Then he met another young lady, and the same thing occurred. One night, he called me crying hysterically, and I could hear the alarm and hurt in his voice. I knew that God was in the midst of his situation so I had peace. He wanted to come home and be with his family but he was about an hour and a half away. He acknowledged that he had made some very bad choices, and I was so grateful to God for how He kept him and showed Himself.

Bry admitted that he saw how God was covering him because he would be with his friends at the wrong place, at the wrong time. He admitted God's presence as he was in several situations where his friends would get into trouble and he would not. He shared that he had been experimenting with prescription drugs, drinking, and smoking marijuana. He went on to admit that he had mistreated a young lady he had been intimate with. I encouraged him to seek the Lord and I explained to him that the Lord wanted a relationship with him just like He had with me.

The Lord led me to pray intensely over this situation between Bry and Avery, instructing me to break bondages and addictions. He continued to see her and eventually he called and said that he wanted to come home and bring Avery with him. He mentioned that needed to talk to the whole family. When they arrived, we sat down and listened to what he had to say. It turned out that she was pregnant and her parents already knew. They not only wanted her to have an abortion, but they called her a whore and degraded her. Both she and Bry were visibly hurt and confused. We loved on her and let her know that we would be there for the both of them, regardless of the decision she made. She was in such deep turmoil because of the way her parents were treating her. Bry moved in with her hoping to help her, but that only made matters worse.

Her parents came to visit her and she was in a bad state. She was not eating and she and Bry were not getting along. Things between Bry and her were rocky, to say the least. She told Bry to leave so that she could go to the bar with a friend. He granted her wish and left. He then ended up drinking, and even worse, driving. He called me the next day and said that his passenger side window was busted out, and that he had it replaced on his own. When this happened, he said that he had seen his entire life flash before his eyes. The Lord showed him a vision and in it, he died. Also in the vision, we, his family, were suffering. He had no recollection of how the window had shattered, but he was not hurt. God was working and getting Bry's attention, and I thanked Him for it.

Eventually, Bry and his girlfriend separated but then tried to rekindle their relationship. They were scheduled to go to have a sonogram done, but she canceled the appointment and rescheduled it without telling him. He was very upset because he did not have the opportunity to go. After he got off work the next day, he texted her but did not get a response. When he could not reach her at her job, he tried calling the hospital's emergency department, and again had no success. During this time, the Lord had shown me a vision of the baby while I was in prayer. It was a boy and he had dark hair and blue eyes. In his continuous effort to get ahold of Avery, Bry sent his girlfriend's mother a text. She later responded to his text, telling him that Avery lost the baby. He called me and said, "It's gone." I heard what Bry said, but I felt in my spirit that she terminated the pregnancy. Avery had told us that her parents were very controlling and were against her having the baby from the very beginning. No one knew where Avery was and no one called or communicated with us. I told Bry to leave that place immediately so he reached out my dad and step mom. They comforted him and went to help him pack and bring him home. When they got there, he had changed his mind and decided to stay there. He wanted me to come and stay with him but the Lord would not allow me to go into that environment. As much as I wanted to be there for my son, I just could not go against the Lord this time. He finally did decide to come home the next day, where we found him very depressed. We all rallied around him and nurtured him with love, support. We assured him that the Lord would heal him from this devastating hurt. Eventually, Avery called Bry and explained to him that she lost the baby and almost lost her own life too. We were all hurt by this, but in the midst of it all, God gave me peace and joy. I knew that His Perfect Plan was being performed and that I would spend eternity with my grandson when the time was right.

Write the Vision

God has an awesome way of giving us glimpses of hope and encouragement in the midst of the storms we go through. As Bry was going through his process, the business and the ministry were growing in leaps and bounds. The Lord had been dealing with me about writing a book for quite some time. During this season, He began to send multiple witnesses to confirm His Will concerning it. As I sought the Lord for direction and clarity, He let me know that writing this book was an assignment that would cause me to be stretched in a way that would be challenging and uncomfortable. I realized that I needed to go through this process so that He could use me to heal masses of people and call the nation back to Him. The Lord let me know from the very start, that birthing this book would be a journey that would be painful, but necessary in order for Him to remove the residue and dross from my life. I was willing to submit to His process and continuously confessed that His will and plan would be done in my life and that His thoughts and plans are better than mine. The moment I began to allow Him to start the process, He began to show me.

I was determined to be set free from bitterness and forgiveness. Many times, I felt such heaviness that I thought I would die, and that's exactly what God wanted me to do. He wanted me to die to myself. He allowed the heaviness to push me into a place where I would yield completely to Him. The Holy Spirit continued to encourage me to stand and be faithful in getting this work done. One night, the Lord showed me a dream, and in it I was standing in front of a crowd of people. I asked Him what we were doing there, and He said, "You are going to preach."

I said, "Preach? What am I going to preach? Lord I am not a preacher."

He said, "You are going to tell the people what I have done for you and what I've brought you out of."

It was so real. In fact it was so real that in my dead sleep, I jumped up shouting and praising the Lord, blessing His name. The Lord continuously sent confirmation about the book, reiterating the importance of sharing my testimony.

When God promises something, part of the challenge for us as believers is to focus on what He has said rather than what we see with our natural eyes. Such was the case with Bry. He was battling depression, and his drinking did not help one bit. One night, he went to a bar with a friend. The Lord told me to pray over him with the Blood of Jesus. An hour later, he called, but he could not hear me. His phone disconnected and when I tried to get him back, I couldn't. I tried to call his friend, but his phone went straight to voicemail. A few minutes later, a police officer called and said that he had Bry in his custody and that he was alright. The officer added that he was quite intoxicated, but cooperative and that he was a complete gentleman. By God's Grace, he saw no reason to detain him. He went on to ask me if I could come and get him. Miles and I went to get him from the side of the road where the officer had pulled them over. When we arrived, the officer informed us that if he hadn't stopped Bry and his friend, they would have never made it home. He had followed them and watched them from a distance for quite some time. He watched them drive down the road and almost hit a guardrail. The cop said he had no other choice but to pull them over. Bry's friend was taken to jail before we had got there to pick up Bry. This is the third incident where Bry was in a car with intoxicated friends and they were arrested, but he wasn't.

Bry was extremely drunk like the officer said, and Miles and I went to get his car. We waited until the next day to talk with him, where I confronted him about his behavior and let him know that it was absolutely not acceptable. He should never have allowed his friends to drive drunk. I warned him that he needed to straighten his life up and that God was giving him the same warnings. I also encouraged him and mentioned to him that he was accountable for the example he was setting for his little sister. As we allowed the Lord to use us to minister him, we saw his brokenness. I saw myself in him and recognized his hurt immediately. He was going through the very same things that I experienced when I battled substance abuse in my past. As a parent, it was hard for me to watch my son go through all of this. But, God kept sending people to show me His Love. I had to let go and step back so that He could have free course to handle the situation. I wanted to step in and fix Bry like I knew how, but the Lord assured me that He had everything in control and that everything would be fine.

Let the Dead Bury Their Dead

After all the hurt and turmoil that I had experienced with my family, I deeply desired to reconcile with my step-mom, Dad, my sister Lynn, and my brother Neal. So much time had passed, and I longed for fellowship with them. Bry had been in communication with them since the incident with Avery. He was friends with them on Facebook, so I added them to my Facebook page again. Everyone communicated with each other, but I always felt excluded. I began to really notice that no one ever reached out to me. This was a trick of the enemy to hinder the progress that I was making in my walk with the Lord. It hurt, but I was obedient when the Lord told me to 'unfriend' them in the first place. Below is the letter the Lord gave me to write to my Dad, Lynn, Neal, and my Step-Mom:

"I want you and the family to know that I love you all, but God has been dealing with me on many things. One of them is my family and how I need to let Him lead me with each of you. When I added you back on FB, I stepped out of the way of what God really needed from me. If you are not careful, people will mess you up! We blame the devil for a lot of things that he has nothing to do with. It is not always the devil that has messed a lot of Christians up; it is the people that they associate with. People will mess with your anointing; they will stop your blessings, and even keep you from reaching your next level of destiny."

Here is a prophetic Word of confirmation that the Lord sent through Prophet Sylvester Ofori on Facebook:

There are four kinds of people. There are people who add to your life and there are those who subtract. There are people who divide, and then there are those who multiply. Remove the people who subtract and divide. They will slow your progress and possibly even stop you from becoming what God has destined for you to become. It is time for you to re-evaluate and see if the people around you can handle what God is about to do in your life.

How will they respond when you enter into the next level of destiny? Just because someone says they are with you today does not mean they will be with you tomorrow. There are people who may tell you they love you today, but that does not mean the will not turn against you tomorrow.

At the same time, my relationship with Chloe was changing after the 20 years that I had known her. She started to veer away from the vision of the health and wellness business and the team leadership plan that was set in place. She began to lie and gossip, and I didn't want to see the team fall apart. My life was being tremendously blessed by being a part of the company, but the Lord let me know that there was going to be changes. He said that newness was coming and that I was to move forward. He also said that the ship was sinking and that I needed to jump ship. I was determined that fear and quitting were not options for me. I knew that God was going to use my life to change other people's lives, and I was ready to see His Power at work in me.

Out of the Ashes

Ashes are the residue or ruins that are derived from something that has been destroyed. Whatever has been burned leaves ashes behind so that the former beauty and original state is forever gone. As I look back on the path that my life has taken, I can truly say that not only was God there every step of the way, but He allowed me to experience the fire of being entrapped and bound in a prison of sin and pain. Although the enemy tried to burn me alive, the Love of God through the Lord Jesus Christ, resurrected me, gave me a new life, and empowered me to take my rightful place as a Child of the King!

Throughout this journey, God has used the ashes of my life to teach me valuable lessons. I have learned to be a mother who is determined to pour into her children and speak their destinies into existence according to the Word and Will of God. I am very involved in their lives and encourage them to be the best that they can be. It is my earnest endeavor to be truthful with them and provide them with a peaceful and stable home environment.

My relationship with the Lord has grown in leaps and bounds. Battling addiction taught me that I was powerless to change myself. I needed the Lord's help and guidance in order to be who He wanted me to be and every day I live with that mindset. I am nothing without God and cannot be apart from Him. I thought that the fire of trials in my life would consume me, but I learned the value of separation. In order for me to remain focused on what the Lord was doing in my life and where He was taking me, I had to be removed from distractions. Distractions come through our connections with the wrong people, and can be toxic to your growth and hinder your progress.

The Holy Spirit has done a tremendous work on me as a wife and He is still showing Himself strong in my marriage. As I submitted to His Work, I began to embrace Miles as the headship of our home and family. As wives, we must learn to listen to the Holy Spirit and see our mates as God sees them. We must talk to them the way the Lord would have us to, in spite of how our flesh may feel. We must let go of the brokenness of our pasts, surrender to the working of the Holy Spirit, and allow the Lord to strip us down. I had to humble myself and learn to love the Lord before I could love my husband. Growing up in a violent home placed me at a disadvantage as it pertains to learning what real love is and seeing it in demonstration. I had to be broken in order to be rebuilt and restored again. It is an ongoing process. I still have to check myself before I respond to him in my flesh or try to deal with any situations in the way I feel that they should be handled. I am still learning how to show love and be affectionate toward my husband. Day by day, I am getting better and better with all of these things. I have been blessed with such a loving and compassionate husband who loves me and accepts me for who I am. I am truly blessed and the Lord has done miraculous work on me.

I want to encourage you to seek God, no matter what you're going through. God has you covered and He has a Great Plan for your life. Always look to Him, trust Him only, and believe His word over everything. His word is the final Word and only Word that you should follow. What the enemy means for evil, God will always take and create something beautiful. I challenge you to get up out of the ashes of your past and move toward the Heart of the Father. He is reaching His hand out to you to make the exchange that will transform your life forever. Receive His Love and embrace the awesome destiny He has for you. Give Him your heart and He'll give you His. You shall emerge out of the ashes of your past, in Jesus' Name. You shall live and not die. You are a precious jewel in the Eyes of God. Walk in the power of who He has called you to be. Do not allow the enemy to blind you to the Power of Jesus' Love. Allow Him to turn your nightmare into a fulfilled dream. He is the God who gave everything for you to have His Best, His Grace, His Blessing, and His Beauty, all in exchange for your ashes.

Beauty For Ashes

Written by Miles Burns

Like the rising of the sun starting a new day
From darkness to light, from ashes to beauty
The Lord has anointed you to bring news of riches to the poor
To make whole the brokenhearted, to proclaim freedom to the
captive
Setting free those who are bound
To proclaim the acceptable year of the Lord
Now your story has been shared to all
Overcoming many things so you can hear His Call
Amazing is the grace he has made available to us
Once we've come to the place where we can only submit and
trust
Remember His Love surpasses all understanding
Carrying us through this life, so demanding
To bring us from the pit to the palace is our Father's Plan
So in His Righteousness, we must firmly stand
Glory and honor to our Lord Jesus
May His Holy Spirit continue to teach us
Beauty for ashes, such a lovely thing
All made possible by Jesus our King

About The Author

La Deema Burns lives in Northern Indiana, where she owns her own home-based health and wellness business. God birthed a ministry through her business about two years ago. Via social media, she shares God's Word, Love, and Encouragement to over 34,000 people daily. She grew up in a small town and lived most of her young childhood on a farm. She is still, to this day, an avid lover of the outdoors. Her hobbies include hiking and gardening, and she loves animals. She and her husband Miles have been married for 20 years and are the proud parents of 2 children: Bryson Lee and Mariska. In her free time she enjoys spending time with her family and friends, going out to movies, and dining. She now looks forward to traveling to where ever God needs her to go at that particular time in her life.

Beauty For Ashes

LaDeema Burns

Mailing Address:
PO Box 126
Twelve Mile, Indiana 46988

Email: burnsfamily55@yahoo.com
Website: www.ladeemaburns.net
Facebook: www.facebook.com/la.deema.burns
Twitter: @ladeemaburns
Instagram: www.instagram.com/ladeemaburns
YouTube: www.youtube.com; Search "Ladeema Burns"

Made in the USA
San Bernardino, CA
17 December 2016